COUNTRY STUDIES

USA

Olly Phillipson
Series Editor: John Hopkin

Heinemann Library
Halley Court, Jordan Hill, Oxford OX2 8EJ
A division of Reed Educational & Professional Publishing Ltd.
Heinemann is a registered trademark of Reed Educational & Professional Publishing Ltd.

OXFORD MELBOURNE AUCKLAND
JOHANNESBURG BLANTYRE
GABORONE IBADAN PORTSMOUTH NH (USA) CHICAGO

First published 1999

03 02 0100 99
10 9 8 7 6 5 4 3 2

British Library Cataloguing in Publication Data
A catalogue record for this book is available from the British Library

Phillipson, Olly
    USA. – (Country studies)
        1. United States – Social conditions – 1980 – – Juvenile literature
        2. United States – History – 1969 – – Juvenile literature
        3. United States – Description and travel – – Juvenile literature
        I. Title
        973'.09' 2

ISBN 0 431 01412 4 (Hardback)
        0 431 01413 2 (Paperback)

Typeset and illustrated by Hardlines, Charlbury, Oxford OX7 3PS
Printed and bound by Mateu Cromo, Spain

Acknowledgements

The publisher would like to thank the following for permission to reproduce copyright material.

Maps and extracts

p.21 D AMWUA logo, courtesy of the Arizona Municipal Water Users Association; **p.23 B** The Independent, 15 July 1993, 16 July 1993, 20 July 1993, 28 October 1993 (headlines); **p.24 A** Everglades National Park (logo).

Photos

p.4 A Geosphere Project/Planetary Visions/Science Photo Library; **p.5 B** The Stock Market Photo Library; **p.5 C** S.B. Nace/Panos Pictures; **p.7 B** The Stock Market Photo Library; **p.7 C** The Stock Market Photo Library; **p.7 D** The Stock Market Photo Library; **p.7 E** The Stock Market Photo Library; **p.9 E** Corbis/Tom Bean; **p.11 C** Corbis/Library of Congress; **p.11 D** e.t archive; **p.13 B** Federal Emergency Management Agency; **p.14 A** Rex Features; **p.15 D** The Stock Market Photo Library; **p.16 A** NOAA/Science Photo Library; **p.17 B** Sipa Press/Rex Features; **p.18 A** Corbis/Mar Garanger; **p.18 B** Jim Gipe/Agstock/Science Photo Library; **p.21 E** Corbis/Buddy Mays **p.23 B** Rob Visser/ Environmental Images; **p.26 B** The Stock Market Photo Library; **p.27 E** The Stock Market Photo Library; **p.28 B** The Stock Market Photo Library; **p.31 C** Network/Christopher Pillitz;.**p.31 D** The Stock Market Photo Library; **p.33 C** Liba Taylor/Panos Pictures; **p.34 A** Sipa Press/Rex Features; **p.35 B** Earth Satellite Corporation/Science Photo Library; **p.36 B** The Stock Market Photo Library; **p.39 C** Camera Press; **p.39 D** Corbis; **p.40 D** The Stock Market Photo Library; **p.43 C** Corbis/Charles E. Rotkin; **p.43 D** Corbis/Ed Young; **p.44 B** The Stock Market Photo Library; **p.46 B** Martin Bond/Environmental Images **p.47 C** The Stock Market Library; **p.48 C** Sam Kittner/Panos Pictures; **p.48 E** Rex Features; **p.50 B** The Stock market Photo Library; **p.50 C** The Stock Market Picture Library; **p.52 C** Andrew Hill/Hutchinson Library; **p.55 C** Sipa Press/Rex Features; **p.57 C** The Stock Market Library; **p.57 C** The Stock Market Photo Library; **p.57 C** The Stock Market Photo Library; **p.58 A** The Stock Market Photo Library; **p.58 D** The Stock Market Photo Library

Contents

1 Introducing the USA

The big country	4–5
Empty spaces	6–7
Natural divisions	8–9
Pioneer nation	10–11

2 Environment and hazards

Earthquakes	12–13
Volcanoes	14–15
Hurricanes and tornadoes	16–17
Turning the desert green – the Colorado river	18–19
Investigation: Providing water for Phoenix	20–21
Investigation: Controlling the Mississippi	22–23
Investigation: Protecting Florida's shrinking wetlands	24–25

3 People and cities

Population patterns and structure	26–27
A multicultural country – the 'melting pot'	28–29
On the move	30–31
Migration across the Mexican border	32–33
Investigation: Los Angeles (1) Growth and development	34–35
Investigation: Los Angeles (2) Traffic and transport	36–37
Investigation: Los Angeles (3) Quality of life	38–39

4 Economic development

Industrial change and development	40–41
The rise of the industrial north east	42–43
The changing car industry	44–45
Investigation: Industries of the Sun Belt: California	46–47
Energy and the economy	48–49
Farming in the USA – agribusiness	50–51
Trade and globalization	52–53

5 Comparing regions

Alaska: wilderness versus wealth?	54–55
Florida: the USA's 'Sunshine State'	56–57
New York City and State	58–59

Statistics	60–61
Glossary	62–63
Index	64

1 INTRODUCING THE USA

The big country

▶ **What are the USA's landscapes?**

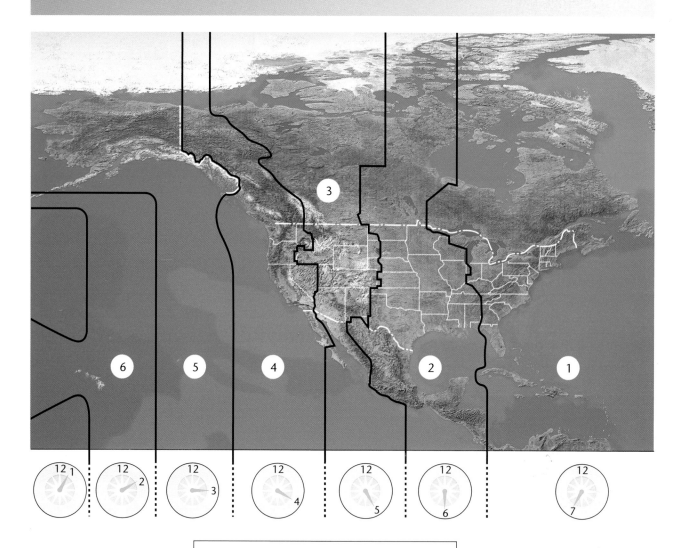

1	EST (Eastern Standard Time)
2	CST (Central Standard Time)
3	MST (Mountain Standard Time)
4	PST (Pacific Standard Time)
5	ASJ (Alaskan Standard Time)
6	HAST (Hawaiian/Aleutian Standard Time)

A A satellite image of the USA. Note the number of time zones across the fifty states.

A giant nation

The USA is the fourth largest country in the world. Its sheer size, including Alaska and Hawaii, takes it through six time zones. Its scenery and climate range from high snow-covered mountains, through lowland river basins and dramatic coastlines to hot, dry deserts. Vast, almost empty spaces contrast with the crowded cities located mainly along its coasts and borders. The two outlying states of Alaska and Hawaii, one permanently frozen, the other constantly changing through volcanic activity, add to the geographical diversity of the country.

B A crowded street in New York

C Monument Valley, Arizona

FACT FILE

Diverse landscapes

The satellite picture opposite clearly shows a number of the USA's diverse physical features. In the Pacific Ocean to the west of mainland USA lie the volcanic islands of Hawaii. To the north west are the frozen lands of Alaska, close to the semi-permanent ice flows of the Artic Circle.

Several important mountain ranges can be seen – including the Rocky Mountains, stretching from Canada, inland from the west coast. The Appalachian Mountains across to the east, south of the Great Lakes form part of the USA's northern border with Canada. Jutting out on the eastern edge of the Gulf of Mexico in the south is the Florida peninsula.

Empty spaces

▶ What are some of the USA's main natural attractions?

Tourists to the USA from overseas and from within the country are attracted by the huge range of landscape, scenery and activities. People visit the vast National Parks such as Yosemite and Yellowstone in search of wildlife. They look at the Earth's geological history through the rock layers at the Grand Canyon; enjoy winter sports in the Rocky Mountains; lie on the beaches at Florida Keys or are deafened by the roar of the water at Niagara Falls. Even with a lot of time and money, it would be difficult to plan an itinerary to take in all of these natural yet contrasting features which make up the USA.

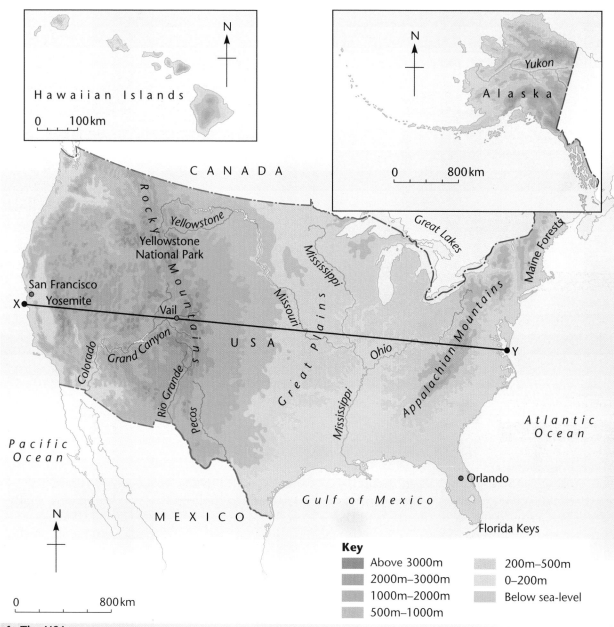

Hawaiian Islands

0   100km

N

Alaska

Yukon

0   800km

CANADA

Rocky Mountains

Yellowstone
Yellowstone National Park

Great Lakes

Maine Forests

San Francisco
Yosemite

X

Vail

Grand Canyon

Colorado

Rio Grande

Pecos

Mississippi

Missouri

USA

Great Plains

Ohio

Appalachian Mountains

Y

Mississippi

Atlantic Ocean

Pacific Ocean

N

MEXICO

Gulf of Mexico

Orlando

Florida Keys

Key

Above 3000m	200m–500m
2000m–3000m	0–200m
1000m–2000m	Below sea-level
500m–1000m	

0   800km

B The Grand Canyon, Colorado

C Yellowstone National Park, Wyoming

The Grand Canyon was carved by the Colorado river over thousands of years through countless layers of sedimentary rock. The sight of this magnificent chasm is hard to do justice to in words and pictures. Enjoy the spectacle from the many paths and viewing points or take a helicopter tour for the ultimate experience.

Yellowstone National Park, Wyoming, is America's first and largest national park, a 3400 square mile wonder of nature at its most spectacular. You will see the stupendous waterfall, Mammoth Hot Springs, geyser basins and the hourly blow of 'Old Faithful'.

Vail, Colorado has some of the best skiing in the world. Set amongst spectacular scenery it gives visitors some of the most breathtaking views of the magnificent Rocky Mountains.

Travelling south, Highway 1 begins a spectacular 110 mile journey across a turquoise sea and a chain of beautiful little islands which make up **Florida Keys**. Each has its own special charm and character – offbeat, laid back and friendly.

D Vail, Colorado

E Florida Keys

FACT FILE

National Parks

The USA's first National Park was Yellowstone, which opened in 1872. Today, the National Parks are run by the National Parks Service (NPS), a bureau for the Department of the Interior. The NPS was created by President Woodrow Wilson on 25 August 1916.

The NPS is currently responsible for 376 separate sites covering 325 000km^2 in nearly every state. They are divided into 20 categories, including the 54 National Parks. There are also monuments, battlefields, military parks, historical parks, historic sites, lake shores, sea shores, recreation areas, scenic rivers and trails and even the White House in Washington D.C.

The main aim of the NPS is to conserve and manage these sites, providing access for the public whilst not damaging them. There are ten regional offices throughout the USA. New areas have to be agreed by Congress.

Natural divisions

▶ How does climate and natural vegetation vary?

The USA stretches over 4500km east to west and 2500km north to south (not including Alaska and Hawaii). This great size results in a wide range of climate and vegetation across the USA. Maps **A** and **B** show the main divisions.

Different climates
There are great differences in the range of temperatures found, especially when comparing coastal areas to inland areas. Along the West

Coast, temperatures vary as little as 10°C over the year; the **maritime** influence creates cooler summer and warmer winter temperatures. As you move inland, **continental** influences take over. Towards the north in the central areas of the USA, the **temperature range** increases to over 30°C, with very hot summers and very cold winters. The East Coast is generally cooler than the West Coast in both summer and winter.

The Cascade and Sierra Nevada mountains close to the West Coast have helped to create the large area of desert and semi-desert in the west of the country (see map **A**). This area sits in a rain shadow. Rain blown from the Pacific

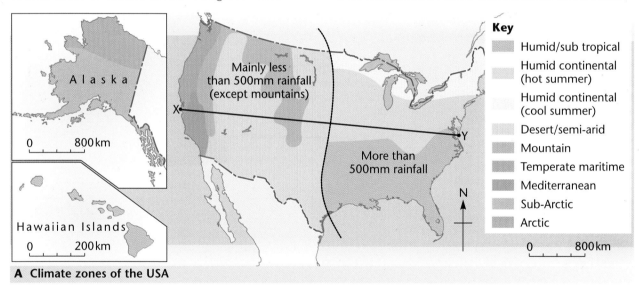

A Climate zones of the USA

Key
- Humid/sub tropical
- Humid continental (hot summer)
- Humid continental (cool summer)
- Desert/semi-arid
- Mountain
- Temperate maritime
- Mediterranean
- Sub-Arctic
- Arctic

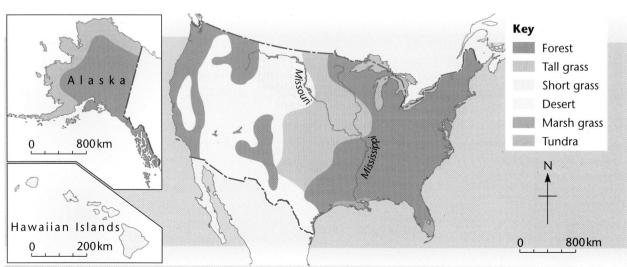

B Vegetation map of the USA

Key
- Forest
- Tall grass
- Short grass
- Desert
- Marsh grass
- Tundra

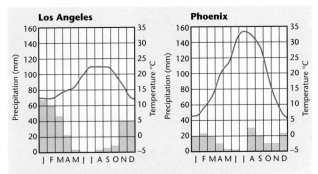

C Climate graphs for Los Angeles and Phoenix

E Natural grasslands of the Central Plains

New York	Precipitation											
	mm	84	79	99	93	106	85	105	104	91	84	107	92
	Temperature											
	°C	0	1	6	11	17	22	25	24	20	14	9	3
New Orleans	Precipitation											
	mm	126	133	120	114	129	118	171	153	149	68	103	134
	Temperature											
	°C	13	14	16	19	23	25	26	26	24	20	15	14
		J	F	M	A	M	J	J	A	S	O	N	D

D Climate data for New York City and New Orleans

Ocean in the west falls on the high ground, creating a wide rain shadow area inland. This means that, away from the Pacific coast, almost half the country receives less than 500mm of rain per year. This contrasts with the entire eastern half of the USA where between 500 and 1500mm falls per year. The 500mm rainfall lines divide the wetter farmlands of the east from the drier lands to the west, where farmers depend on irrigation.

Natural vegetation

Patterns of natural vegetation (see map **B**) are closely linked to climate. Over most of the eastern half of the USA, mixed temperate forests once grew, although today much has been cleared for farming, settlement and industry. In the central areas west of the Mississippi–Missouri river basin, woodland gave way to the tall grasses of the Prairies. As the rainfall lessened towards the west, grasses became shorter and thinner until vegetation almost disappeared completely. On the Pacific coast of the north west, dense forests still cover the slopes of the mountains, fed by heavy rains from the west. Amongst these forests are some of the world's oldest trees – thousands of years old.

FACT FILE

Climatic contrasts

Highest temperature by state

Location	State	Temperature °C	Date
Greenland Ranch	California	55	10 July 1913
Lake Havusu City	Arizona	53	29 June 1994
Laughlin	Nevada	52	29 June 1994

Lowest temperature by state

Location	State	Temperature °C	Date
Prospect Creek	Alaska	−27	23 January 1971
Rogers Pass	Montana	−21	20 January 1954
Peters Sink	Utah	−20.5	1 February 1985

Maximum precipitation (24 hours) by state

Location	State	Precipitation (mm)	Date
Alvin	Texas	1092	25/26 July 1979
Yankeetown	Florida	983	5 September 1950
Kilauea plantation	Hawaii	965	24/25 January 1956

Pioneer nation

Much of the USA was sparsely populated or uninhabited as recently as 150 years ago. As the country was opened up, so the population grew as many people emigrated to this 'New World' in search of a better life.

In the beginning

The original people of the USA are the Native Americans. By the 1600s many Native American tribes had moved to the Great Plains, riding horses and hunting bison. Gradually, explorers and colonists from Britain, France, Spain and Portugal 'discovered' this vast country, taking land to farm and settle.

Between 1600 and 1800 over a million people from Africa were captured by British, Spanish and Portuguese traders and forcibly taken to North America as slaves. They were forced to work on the cotton and tobacco plantations in the south. Demand for labour was high, and by 1790 black slaves made up 20 per cent of the USA's population.

Year	Population (millions)	Year	Population (millions)
1800	5.5	1900	81
1810	10	1910	100
1820	12	1920	112
1830	17	1930	130
1840	19	1940	137
1850	27	1950	158
1860	38	1960	181
1870	45	1970	205
1880	55	1980	226
1890	68	1990	248

A Population growth of the USA

In 1776 the USA declared its independence from Britain. There were then only thirteen States, all in the east. Most of the centre and the west of the country had been explored only by Spanish colonists from Mexico. Eighty years later pioneer Americans crossed from the east to the central plains and deserts, over the Rocky Mountains to the West Coast. The final push westwards was largely the result of the expansion of the railways and the promise of riches during the Californian Gold Rush of 1849.

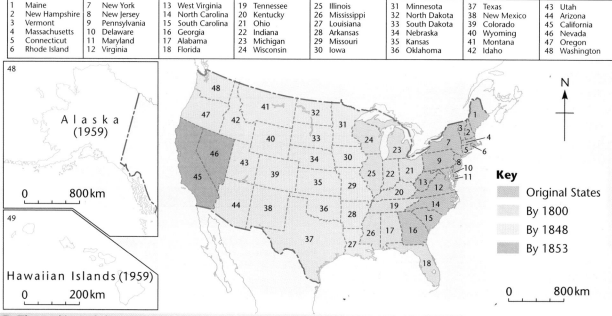

1 Maine	7 New York	13 West Virginia	19 Tennessee	25 Illinois	31 Minnesota	37 Texas	43 Utah
2 New Hampshire	8 New Jersey	14 North Carolina	20 Kentucky	26 Mississippi	32 North Dakota	38 New Mexico	44 Arizona
3 Vermont	9 Pennsylvania	15 South Carolina	21 Ohio	27 Louisiana	33 South Dakota	39 Colorado	45 California
4 Massachusetts	10 Delaware	16 Georgia	22 Indiana	28 Arkansas	34 Nebraska	40 Wyoming	46 Nevada
5 Connecticut	11 Maryland	17 Alabama	23 Michigan	29 Missouri	35 Kansas	41 Montana	47 Oregon
6 Rhode Island	12 Virginia	18 Florida	24 Wisconsin	30 Iowa	36 Oklahoma	42 Idaho	48 Washington

Alaska (1959)

0   800km

Hawaiian Islands (1959)

0   200km

Key
- Original States
- By 1800
- By 1848
- By 1853

0   800km

B The making of the USA

C A gang of slaves on their way to be sold

D A Native American group hunting buffalo

While the West Coast gradually became settled, towns in the east grew rapidly. The large rise in population was largely fuelled by high levels of immigration. In 1800 the population of the USA was about 5.5 million. This increased dramatically as millions came first from western Europe, then later from eastern Europe and Asia. By the end of the nineteenth century 30 million new immigrants had settled in the USA.

The twentieth century

Between 1900 and 1910 a further nine million people emigrated to the USA. Since then the country's population has more than doubled. This huge influx of people and the movement across the USA had a disastrous effect on the Native American people. They once numbered many millions but less than two million now survive. Most were forced off their tribal homelands and scattered throughout the north and central parts of the USA into much smaller reservations.

Other groups have also suffered. Although slavery was abolished in 1865, African Americans living in the southern states of the USA continued to be treated as second-class citizens. In the 1960s, pressure from Civil Rights groups brought about changes to outlaw discrimination, although many African Americans continue to face discrimination.

Today the USA is made up of 50 states, 48 on mainland USA, plus Alaska to the north west and Hawaii to the west. Increasingly, immigrants come from Mexico and other Spanish-speaking countries to the south, and from the countries of south-east Asia to the west. The total population is now more than 260 million.

FACT FILE·

Dr Martin Luther King

Born in 1929, King was a clergyman and one of the USA's most influential Civil Rights leaders. A black American from Atlanta, many of his ideas were based on the work of Mohandas Gandhi. In 1955 he led a boycott of bus services in Montgomery following the arrest of Rosa Parks, a black woman who had broken the law by refusing to give up her seat to a white person. King was put in jail, but by the following year segregation by race on public transport was prohibited.

In 1963 King led a huge Civil Rights campaign in Alabama and was arrested more than once. In August 1963 he made his famous speech:

'I have a dream…my four little children may one day live in a nation where they will not be judged by the colour of their skin but by the content of their character …I have a dream today.'

A year later he was awarded the Nobel Prize for Peace. On 4 April 1968, the day after he said in a speech that he had 'been to the mountain top and seen the promised land', he was shot dead in Memphis by James Earl Ray. Since 1983 a national holiday has been held on his birthday in January in his honour.

2 ENVIRONMENT AND HAZARDS

Earthquakes

▶ Why are earthquakes so common along the Pacific coast?
▶ What were the effects – and lessons – of the 1994 Los Angeles earthquake?

The San Andreas fault

The Earth's crust is broken up into large sections called **plates**. As these plates move above the molten rock, which lies beneath the crust, they create earthquakes, volcanic activity and great mountain ranges. Most of the world's earthquakes occur along the lines where plates meet. These lines are called **faults**. One of the best known is the San Andreas fault, which runs along the USA's Pacific coast.

The San Andreas fault forms the boundary between the Pacific Plate to the west and the North American Plate to the east (see diagram A). This fault, plus several smaller faults, stretches over 1600km and reaches a depth of 15km. The zones of crushed, broken rocks found along the faults are caused by the Pacific Plate moving north west past the North American Plate by about 5cm per year. These plates are stationary for long periods of time. When they do move, they slide past one another, and earthquakes or earth tremors occur. This type of fault is called a **transform fault** and the

plate boundary is called a **conservative margin**. There is no volcanic activity along this type of fault.

**A The San Andreas fault –
plates and their relative movement**

LOS ANGELES EARTHQUAKE, 1994

On 17 January 1994 at 4.31 am an earthquake measuring 6.7 on the Richter scale shook Los Angeles. Its **epicentre** was in Northridge, 30km north west of Los Angeles. Although a strong (not major) earthquake, it was one of the USA's worst natural disasters, causing $15 billion of damage to buildings alone. It hit a densely populated part of the San Fernando Valley, killing 57 people and seriously injuring over a thousand. About 25 000 people were left homeless, 150 000 without water, 20 000 without gas and 10 000 without

electricity. Seven major freeways suffered damage and a number of bridges collapsed.

Most of the damage was caused by the initial earthquake, but fires and a series of aftershocks added to the problems. Fortunately the earthquake happened early in the morning when few people were at work or on the roads. Even so, thousands of buildings were destroyed or seriously damaged and disruption to traffic lasted many months.

An ever-present threat

Lessons have been learned from previous earthquakes. Newer structures and buildings conform to a strict new code aimed at reducing loss of life. Many of the buildings which survived the 1994 Los Angeles earthquake had been strengthened or built according to the new guidelines.

For the millions of people living on or near the San Andreas fault line along the USA's Pacific coast, the earthquake **hazard** is an ever-present threat. Scientists predict that sooner or later the 'Big One' will hit. Despite new, safer buildings and high-tech monitoring, no-one knows when or where this might happen in an area which is very densely populated.

B Earthquake damage, Northridge, Los Angeles, January 1994

Location	Date	Magnitude	Deaths	Damage
San Francisco	18 April 06	8.35	700-3000	$500 million
Imperial Valley (Mexican border)	22 June 15	6.2	6	$1 million
Santa Barbara	29 June25	6.3	13	$8 million
Long Beach	11 March 33	6.3	115	$40 million
Imperial Valley	19 May 40	7.1	9	$6 million
Kern County	21 July 52	6.2	12	$60 million
Coalinga	2 May 83	6.4	0	
Loma Prieta (SF)	17 October 89	7.1	63	$6 billion
Northridge (LA)	17 January 94	6.7	57	$15 billion

C Major Californian earthquakes in the 20th century

FACT FILE
Most powerful US earthquakes

	Location	Date	Force
1	Prince William Sound, Alaska	1964	9.2
2	Andreanof Islands, Alaska	1957	8.8
3	Rat Islands, Alaska	1965	8.7
4	East of Shumagin Islands, Alaska	1938	8.3
5	Lituya Bay, Alaska	1958	8.3
6	Yakutat Bay, Alaska	1899	8.2
7	Near Cape Yakataga, Alaska	1899	8.2
8	Andreanof Islands, Alaska	1986	8.0
9	New Madrid, Missouri	1812	7.9
10	Fort Tejon, California	1857	7.9

Earthquake defence
No-one can stop earthquakes – people have to learn to live with them, especially if they live near a plate boundary, like many Californians. Certain precautions can be taken though. In cities like San Francisco all new buildings have to be 'earthquake proof' and able to resist collapsing when the ground shakes. Areas of major hazard, such as the San Andreas fault itself, should not be built on. In the future scientists hope that accurate prediction will help save lives. The US Geological Survey and other such groups have been working for 20 years to improve prediction rates and minimise potential hazards.

Volcanoes

▶ How are the volcanic eruptions of Mount St Helens and Kilauea different?

A Mount St Helens erupting

Mount St Helens

The previous two pages show how vulnerable the West Coast of the USA is to earthquakes. Volcanic activity is also common in this part of the USA. The eruption of Mount St Helens in 1980 was one of the first major world eruptions to be filmed as it happened. Despite months of warnings, over 50 people died and a large area of Washington State was devastated. This was partly because the eruption came as a sudden explosion, and partly because the blast travelled sideways as the mountain collapsed. The heat from the volcano caused snow and ice to melt, sweeping soil and rock into rivers and turning them into fast-flowing torrents of mud. Trees over 50km away were flattened and stripped of their branches. Ash released into the atmosphere affected the world's weather patterns for several years afterwards. Mount St Helens is a **composite volcano** (see diagram C).

Hawaii and the Kilauea volcano

Hawaii owes its entire existence to volcanic activity. The 800 large islands and hundreds of small islands of the state are the tops of a series of volcanoes that rise up from the floor of the Pacific Ocean. They stretch over 2000km from east to west, just south of the Tropic of Cancer. The islands have taken thousands of years to form, as successive outpourings of lava have built up from a depth of 6000m below sea level to over 4000m above it.

Only two Hawaiian volcanoes are still active today – Mauna Loa and Kilauea. Both are shield type volcanoes on the island of Hawaii itself. **Shield volcanoes** (see diagram C) build up slowly as lava escapes to the surface, not dramatically in great explosions. Kilauea, a large crater on the slopes of Mauna Loa, is the most active volcano in the world. The crater is only about 1100m above sea level, but its walls reach over 200m in height and it covers an area of 10km². Lava constantly pours out onto the surface in **effusive** eruptions at a rate of almost 400 000m³ per day (see map **B**).

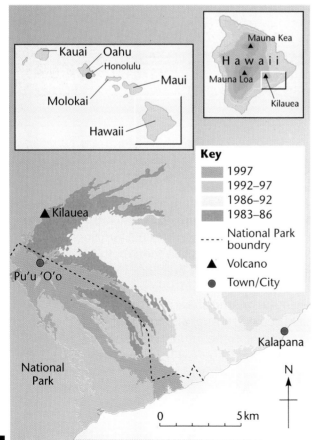

Key

- 1997
- 1992–97
- 1986–92
- 1983–86
- National Park boundry
- ▲ Volcano
- ● Town/City

0   5km

N

B Most recent lava flows on Hawaii

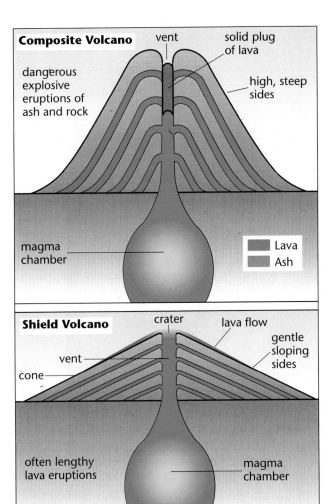

Composite Volcano vent — solid plug of lava

dangerous explosive eruptions of ash and rock

high, steep sides

magma chamber

■ Lava
■ Ash

Shield Volcano crater — lava flow

gentle sloping sides

vent

cone

often lengthy lava eruptions

magma chamber

C Composite and shield volcanoes

Although lava generally pours out slowly, the damage caused over the years has been considerable. Kilauea has been erupting continuously since January 1983. It has destroyed 181 homes and numerous other buildings, roads and tracks, plus many important archaeological sites. The total cost of this eruption so far is estimated at $61 million. As the lava has cooled, it has created over 200 hectares of new land.

Volcanic activity on Hawaii has been closely observed by scientists since an observatory was set up on the rim of Kilauea in 1912. This study has greatly helped our understanding of how the Earth was – and is continuing to be – formed.

D Mount Kilauea

FACT FILE

Mount St Helens
Until the devastating eruption on 18 May 1980 Mount St Helens had been dormant for 123 years. Before the eruption it measured 2950m. Afterwards the top 400m were missing and a new crater 3km long had appeared on the remains of its northern face. Ash from the eruption rose almost 20km into the atmosphere, disrupting weather patterns and increasing the amount of reflected energy.

Mount St Helens is part of the Cascade range of mountains in the north west of the USA. These mountains are volcanic in origin, caused as an oceanic plate to the west slid underneath the continental North American plate. As the oceanic plate is destroyed, magma is pushed up towards the earth's surface, sometimes with explosive results.

▶ **How are hurricanes and tornadoes similar and different?**

A A satellite image of Hurricane Andrew

Hurricanes

Every year, ten to twelve hurricanes form in the western Atlantic Ocean between June and November. Warm tropical water heats the air, causing storms to form. These may develop into tropical storms which track north west towards the USA and the Caribbean. If wind speeds reach over 120km per hour the storm becomes a hurricane. Hurricanes can cause widespread devastation with high winds, torrential rain and storm waves. In the USA, the states along the south and south-east coast are most at risk.

Tornadoes

Only a few hurricanes hit the USA each year compared to about a thousand tornadoes. The USA has more tornadoes than any other country in the world.

HURRICANE ANDREW

In August 1992 Hurricane Andrew hit Florida and Louisiana. Andrew began as a tropical wave west of Africa around 16 August. It moved towards the USA on 17 August and developed into a tropical storm. By 22 August it seemed to be slowing down, but suddenly it changed direction and reached hurricane force with winds of 230km per hour – a category 4 hurricane. These winds, plus tides over 3m higher than normal, hit Florida on 22 August, causing immense damage. Andrew then turned north to hit the Louisiana coast on 26 August. Although weakening, it still brought high winds and torrential rain to the area. By the time it had finished on 28 August, 26 people were dead, 250 000 were homeless and $30 billion of damage had been caused, making Hurricane Andrew the most expensive natural disaster in US history.

Another potentially more devastating hurricane hit the Southern states in September 1998 – Hurricane Georges. Estimates for the damage caused are still incomplete.

They are so common that the area from Nebraska to Texas is called 'Tornado Alley'. Tornadoes develop from thunderstorms and are columns of air, which rotate violently, stretching from the thundercloud to the ground. These thunderclouds can reach over 15 000m in height. Differences in temperature between masses of air cause thunderstorms to form. When warm and cold air meet, air can start to rotate in a spiralling column. As it spins it gets faster, sucking in air and anything in its path.

Tornadoes are classified on a five-point scale (F1 weakest – F5 strongest). Fortunately F5 tornadoes, with winds between 261 and 318km per hour, are rare. In June 1997 an F5 tornado hit the small town of Jarrell, Texas, killing 27 people and causing $25 million of damage as homes were ripped apart and flattened. A tornado warning was issued, but only 18 minutes before it struck Jarrell, and few people had basements to shelter in.

It is relatively easy to monitor the development of hurricanes and to issue warnings before they strike land. Despite widespread damage, deaths and injuries are often quite low. Tornado prediction, however, is much more difficult. While the damage caused is usually over quite small areas, almost a hundred people in the USA are killed by them each year.

B A tornado

Date (5-year periods)	Tornadoes	Deaths
1960–64	3 137	232
1965–69	3 676	710
1970–74	4 331	714
1975–79	4 249	284
1980–84	4 533	272
1985–89	3 663	250
1990–94	5 817	233
Totals		
1960–94	29 406	2695

C Number of tornadoes and deaths, USA, 1960–94

FACT FILE

Naming hurricanes
Hurricanes were first given names in the early 1900s, when an Australian forecaster started naming them after politicians he disliked! Since then the process has become more organized.

Naming is now the responsibility of the World Meteorological Organisation, who vote on names from lists given by member countries. These follow a six-year cycle – so the names for 1997 were first used in 1991. Names given to tropical storms which cause great damage or deaths are 'retired' e.g. Andrew was retired after 1992 and replaced by Alex. The letters Q, U, X, Y and Z are not used as there are not enough names available beginning with these letters.

It wasn't until the late 1970s that the present system of alternating men's and women's names became standard practice. Names are thought to be useful by meteorologists in helping communicate information and warnings about individual hurricanes.

Future hurricane names	
1999	Arlene, Bret, Cindy, Dennis, Emily, Floyd, Gert, Harvey, Irene, Jose, Katrina, Lenny, Maria, Nate, Ophelia, Philippe, Rita, Stan, Tammy, Vince, Wilma
2000	Alberto, Beryl, Chris, Debby, Ernesto, Florence, Gordon, Helene, Isaac, Joyce, Keith, Leslie, Michael, Nadine, Oscar, Patty, Rafael, Sandy, Tony, Valerie, William
2001	Allison, Barry, Chantal, Dean, Erin, Felix, Gabrielle, Humberto, Iris, Jerry, Karen, Lorenzo, Michelle, Noel, Olga, Pablo, Rebekah, Sebastien, Tanya, Van, Wendy

Turning the desert green – the Colorado river

> ▶ **How has technology opened up the deserts of the south west?**

The walls of the spectacular Grand Canyon are formed from many layers of rocks that go back through geological time. They dwarf the river that flows through it. Yet the Colorado river is vital to the seventeen million people who live in some of the hottest and most arid parts of the USA. The Colorado is the only **perennial** (permanent) river flowing through this desert area, which forms almost a third of the USA. Its source is in Wyoming in the Rocky Mountains, and it flows south for 2300km through seven states and Mexico before reaching the sea in the Gulf of Mexico.

A Aerial view of Hoover Dam and Lake Mead

Water from the Colorado

Water has been taken from the Colorado since it was first discovered by the pioneer settlers going west in the early nineteenth century. Today agriculture and the fast-growing cities of the south west owe their very existence to the river. The importance of the Colorado as the major source of water has resulted in numerous dams and reservoirs being built. To regulate construction and use, many laws have been passed, but as demand grows arguments

continue as each state tries to increase its share. Water use is strictly allocated by the Colorado Basin Compact.

There is also conflict between different users of this precious resource. Farmers who try to increase yields by using irrigation, city planners who build more and more homes to keep pace with people moving in from the rest of the country and leisure amenities such as golf courses all demand a share of the water. Colorado water is used to provide twelve billion kW hours of hydroelectric power each year, helping the rapid growth of cities such as Las Vegas and Phoenix. Major reductions in the flow of the river through over-use could affect power supplies.

Irrigation

Agriculture is by far the biggest user of Colorado water. It is used to irrigate 40 000 hectares of farmland in California, Arizona and Nevada. Canals run for hundreds of kilometres, creating man-made oases in the desert. **Capital-intensive**, high-tech farms produce 90 per cent of the USA's fruit and vegetables here during the winter. To turn the desert green takes vast amounts of water, especially as **field** or **flood irrigation** is the most commonly used method. **Sprinkler** and **drip** (trickle) **irrigation** use far less water. Farmers may need to change their methods in future if demand continues to rise.

B Irrigated farmland surrounded by desert

The Colorado is probably the most controlled, managed and regulated river in the world. Parts of the river have almost dried up as water extraction has continued to rise, and water supply continues to fall. Table **D** lists some of the benefits – and disadvantages – that controlling the Colorado has brought. It seems unlikely that current levels of use are sustainable – yet expansion continues.

C The Colorado River Basin and surrounding states

Key
- Upper Colorado River Basin
- Lower Colorado River Basin
- Dams

D Controlling the Colorado river

Benefits

Irrigation – over 400 000 hectares of farmland

Hydroelectric power – 12 billion kW of HEP provided annually

Domestic water supply – to 'desert' towns, e.g. Las Vegas, Tucson and Phoenix

Flooding – dams and reservoirs control flooding, especially in Upper Basin after spring snow melt

Leisure use – water sports on the reservoirs and lakes; irrigation on golf courses and urban landscaping; swimming pools

Disadvantages

Disputes over water rights/allocation

Demand for water outstrips supply

Several Native American tribes have land in the area. Colorado management plans may flood their land.

Fishing and wildlife in the delta have been devastated as little water and sediment now reach it. Sediment is trapped behind dams.

Salinity (salt content) and pollution of water is very high. Desalination plants have had to be built to help Mexican farmers whose yields are falling.

Flood irrigation (still commonly used) is very wasteful.

FACT FILE

The Colorado River

The Colorado's source is in the Rocky Mountains in the north of Colorado State. It flows over 2300km south west into Mexico, entering the sea via the Gulf of Mexico. The river cuts through the surrounding rocks to form the spectacular Grand Canyon, almost 200km long, 10km wide and 1.5km deep.

Although not the USA's longest river, the Colorado is one of the most important, flowing as it does through the arid lands of the western third of the country. The cities and farms of this part of the USA rely almost entirely on water from the Colorado, transported hundreds of kilometres via irrigation canals.

There are 19 major dams on the river controlling its flow and storing water for use all year round. These dams also generate hydro electric power. The most famous is the Hoover dam, built between 1931 and 1936, and named after President Herbert Hoover. At the time it was the largest dam in the world and its reservoir – Lake Mead – is still one of the largest. The dam is over 220m high and almost 380m long. Lake Mead covers 700km². It generates 1.5kw of electricity every year to nearby desert states.

Providing water for Phoenix

▶ **How does Phoenix get its water?**
▶ **How can water be conserved?**

Phoenix, Arizona, is one of the USA's fastest growing cities (see table A). Providing water for its ever-increasing population in a desert region is a huge problem. Almost 500 million gallons are used every day in summer (170 million gallons in winter). Almost 60 per cent of this is from surface water (the Colorado and its tributaries), with 40 per cent from underground sources. Water use is strictly controlled by the Arizona Department of Water Resources (ADWR), whose aim is to secure long-term water supplies for Arizona's communities. It enforces state water supply laws, explores ways of meeting future demands and promotes water conservation.

Groundwater v surface water

ADWR is particularly concerned with the amount of groundwater being used by the expanding cities of Arizona. Groundwater supplies have taken centuries to build up in the rocks below the surface. They are being used far more quickly than they can be replaced by rainfall. The ADWR has created five active management areas (AMAs) in the state. Each one is strictly controlled and aims to reach 'safe-yield' by the year 2025. This means that the total groundwater allowed to be used cannot be more than the amount replaced each year. Over two thirds of Arizona's population lives in Phoenix and it is at the centre of one of these areas (see map C).

Although Phoenix has quickly become an industrial area, farming is still very important and uses vast quantities of water for irrigation. The ADWR is encouraging the use of water from a renewable surface water source using the Colorado river – the Central Arizona Project completed in 1985. Within the Phoenix AMA, some of the largest users of water for agriculture are the Native American communities. There are three groups, at Fort McDowell, the Salt river and Gila river, all holding important water

A Phoenix population figures

Year	Population
1910	11 000
1940	66 000
1950	107 000
1960	440 000
1970	582 000
1980	790 000
1990	950 000
1995	1.2 million

B Water use in Phoenix active management area (AMA), 1994

Agriculture	53%
Municipal (mainly homes)	40%
Industry	7%

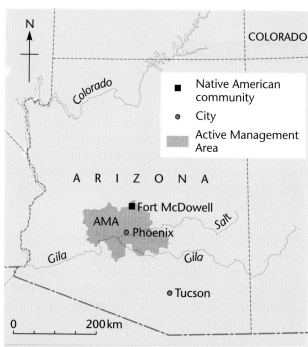

C Phoenix active management area (AMA)

rights. Currently water for farming only costs 25 per cent of the price charged for municipal users. This is partly because farming areas can make more use of renewable supplies, whereas industry and homes are too far away from such supplies and rely heavily on groundwater that the ADWR is trying to conserve.

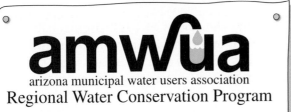

Regional Water Conservation Program

You can use less water in your home if you:

- check taps and pipes for leaks and drips
- don't run water when cleaning teeth or shaving
- use low-flow showers
- use a toilet dam in your cistern (uses less water)
- run dishwashers and washing machines only when full
- wash cars from a bucket, not with a hose
- water lawns every three days and when it is coolest

ADOPT A WATER-WISE LIFESTYLE !

D AMWUA – water conservation advice

Educating for the future

Taking care of limited resources (water in the case of Phoenix) is becoming a major issue for many communities. AMWUA (Arizona Municipal Water Users' Association) is one of the conservation groups set up to help develop water policies for cities such as Phoenix. They also provide advice and information and produce resources for use in schools. They are keen to promote water conservation: *'we live in a desert, water is our most important and precious resource ... we must all do our part to use water wisely.'* Educating both young and old about water conservation is vital if the prosperity of cities such as Phoenix is to continue in the future. Water conservation is very important in the home, given the increase in population and water use.

E Phoenix, Arizona – city in the desert

FACT FILE

Arizona Municipal Water Users Association (AMWUA)

AMWUA was formed as a non-profit making organization in 1969. Educating people and companies in water conservation (see leaflet **D**) is a major part of its work.

Water in Our Desert Community is designed for use by pupils in grades 6–9, supporting curriculum studies on Arizona's environment and raising awareness of the economic, environmental and social impact of water use. The pack includes information on the importance of water; the history of water use in Arizona; local water resources; water treatment, users and conservation; and associated problems and issues.

Farming in Arizona

The main crops grown in Arizona are cotton, oranges, alfalfa and vegetables. All rely on water supplied for irrigation. The main areas for growing these crops are along the Colorado, Salt and Gila rivers and in a number of areas between Tuscon and Phoenix.

Controlling the Mississippi

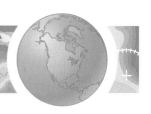

▶ What caused the floods of 1993?

A The Mississippi Basin

The Mississippi is the USA's longest river (see map A). It provides water for homes, agriculture and industry as well as a route for transporting goods and raw materials. Like most rivers it often floods, especially in spring when rainfall is heaviest and temperatures rise, causing snow to melt. When the river floods, fertile silt is deposited over the **flood plain**. However, as the flood plain has become increasingly built up with new settlements, more and more measures have been taken to control the river and prevent flooding.

Flood control

For much of the twentieth century large embankments (called **levées**) have been the main line of defence, gradually being made higher and stronger. These were not strong enough to prevent occasional major floods, as for example in 1927 when the river flooded over 75km each side of its channel. In this flood 217 people died, almost three quarters of a million were temporarily evacuated and there were huge crop and livestock losses.

Following the floods of 1927 engineers tried a number of other ways to prevent future disasters. Hundreds of dams and reservoirs were built on tributaries of the Mississippi; levées were strengthened with concrete; overflow channels were dug to take excess water; and areas (especially in the Tennessee Valley) were reforested in an effort to increase rainfall **interception** and delay surface **run-off**. A number of large **meanders** were straightened, decreasing the length of the river and speeding up the flow of water. To keep the river navigable, **wing dykes** were built along some sections of river, trapping sediment on one side and encouraging erosion and deepening of the river channel on the other.

The 1993 floods

As the headlines show (see opposite), despite all the efforts by engineers the Mississippi floods of 1993 were the worst ever. During the spring, rainfall had been very heavy. As the ground became **saturated**, surface run-off into the river and its tributaries increased. Intense thunderstorms followed in June and July as a high pressure system pushed warm air to the north west. As a result some places experienced more than twice their normal rainfall. Dams began to burst in June and the upper Mississippi and many bridges were closed to river and vehicle traffic. At the height of the disaster over 25 000km² of land was flooded and the President had to declare a state of emergency in nine states. The main effects of the flood are summarized in table C, many being felt for months after the waters receded.

The impact of flood control

Although the main cause of flooding in 1993 was very heavy rainfall, many people argued that efforts to control the Mississippi actually made the floods worse. Straightening the meanders caused the river to flow faster (and, once straightened, the river will try to meander again). Levées restricted the channel causing problems downstream.

'The Father of all floods'
(The Independent, 20 July 1993)

'Ol' Man's Rivers Gloom'
(The Independent, 28 October 1993)

' "Biblical" floods threaten the Midwest'
(The Independent, 15 July 1993)

US unable to tame the Mississippi

As the Great Flood of 1993 continues to wreak havoc across the Mid-western US, a country long accustomed to believing that human technology could solve all problems is beginning to wonder: can people tame the Mississippi river, and indeed should they even try?

The answer to the first part still looked in grave doubt. But increasingly the second question is being posed. *The Chicago Tribune* asked this week "whether the precautions have been worth the cost, or whether they could have made matters worse". Others point out that townships built along the river, and the artificial protection they required, had interfered with a flood's natural function of bringing new fertile topsoil to farmlands. They question the logic of allowing settlements to be built, then paying federal insurance for those who suffer from calamities which are inevitable.

The Independent, 16 July 1993

B Flood damage, 1993

C	The floods of 1993	
	Date	June–July 1993
	Peak discharge	26 June 1993
	Deaths	45
	Evacuated	74 000
	Houses flooded	45 000
	Total damage	$10.5 billion
	Crop damage	$6.5 billion

FACT FILE

Valmeyer, Illinois

Valmeyer was built in 1902, as the railroads reached Illinois. There had been no flooding there during the previous 100 years. However, the floods did come – in 1943, then in 1944 and again in 1947.

After 1947 a new levee was built 3km upstream, protecting Valmeyer from the 1973 floods. The people felt safe – and then came the devastation of 1993.

On 1 August the Mississippi, which was 7m above normal flood levels, broke through the new levee, submerging Valmeyer for a month. As the waters subsided and the clean-up began, a second flood hit on 10 September. This time the 900 residents, their land and houses covered with thick, brown mud and debris, moved out for good. By 1994 land had been bought 117m above the river – the site of the new Valmeyer. Most families moved here, living in caravans nearby whilst the new town was built at a cost of $25 million, paid for by the State and Federal government.

23

Protecting Florida's shrinking wetlands

▶ How can we resolve conflicts of uses in an endangered environment?

Everglades National Park

The Everglades National Park covers the southern half of the **sub-tropical wetlands** that form Florida's Everglades (see map **A** and datafile **B**). The Park's aims are to preserve the flat, low-lying salt and freshwater marshland, thought to be 8000 years old, and its varied plant and animal life.

The wetlands once stretched from Orlando via the Kissimmee river to Lake Okeechobee down to Florida Bay and the Gulf of Mexico, covering an area of 27 000km². As the area has shrunk, threats to the natural ecosystem have increased.

A park in danger

Despite being a National Park, this area is under threat. As the resident population increases and the number of tourists rises, the demand for water and land has risen rapidly. Farming also creates growing demands for water, with a vast network of ditches draining the land. It also pollutes the water as run-off carries animal waste and harmful nitrates and pesticides back into the ecosystem (see table **D**).

Plant and animal communities in the Everglades are uniquely adapted to the natural conditions found here. They rely on the quality and amount of water available. Fresh water comes from rainfall in the Kissimmee river basin from May to October. It flows south from Lake Okeechobee to the sea, feeding the famous 'River of Grass', an area of sawgrass up to 80km wide and between 15 and 90cm deep. Near the coast, salt water mixes with fresh water, supporting different species of plants, animals, insects and birds. Even minor alterations to the flow of water can have far reaching consequences to the complex food chains of the region. The timing of the wet and dry seasons is also critical, especially for migrating birds and animals.

A The Everglades National Park today

Opened	1947
Status	National Park; International Biosphere Reserve and World Heritage Site
Habitat	Freshwater and saltwater marsh/wetland
Trees	120 species, e.g. cypress, pine and mangrove
Plants	Sawgrass, water lilies, orchids, ferns
Birds	300 species, e.g. heron, pelican, kingfisher
Animals	Alligators, panthers, turtles and manatees
Leisure activities	Canoeing, hiking and boardwalks

B Everglades National Park datafile

Action for the future

At the end of the 1980s the National Park sued the state of Florida for its failure to protect the quality of water flowing into the Park. After several years of negotiations the Everglades Forever Act was passed in 1994, setting standards for the future and starting a massive clean-up. A newly formed task force will co-ordinate the restoration programme (see map **C**), which is aimed at protecting the unique environment of the Everglades while sustaining local economies. In 1997 $200 million were set aside by Congress to help with this process.

16 wildlife species including turtles, birds, mammals and butterflies are endangered.
Birdlife has declined by 93 per cent since the 1930s.

Excess nitrates and phosphates in surface run-off from farmland causes **eutrophication** (algae growth) in water.
Toxic mercury accumulations have been discovered in fish.

Natural flows of water are interrupted by a system of canals and **levées**.
Sometimes no water reaches the Park, disrupting the growth of vegetation and affecting the whole food chain.
When released, water floods the Park, and nests and food supplies are washed away.
80 per cent of rainfall is lost via evaporation, transpiration and run-off.
Saltwater flooding from the south (especially during the hurricane season)

Florida's population increases by 900 per day, causing pressure on existing water and land resources.
39 million tourists visit Florida every year (12 million in the rainy season).

D Threats to the Everglades

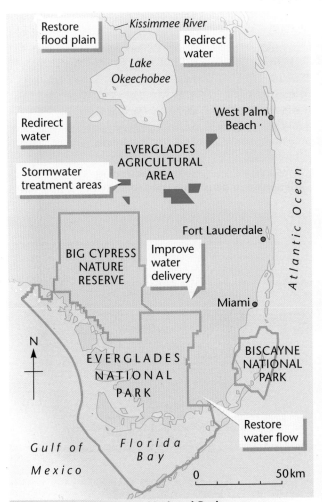

C Proposed changes to National Park

FACT FILE

The Everglades National Park
The establishment of the Everglades National Park was agreed by Congress in 1934, but a range of problems meant that it was 1947 before it opened. In 1976 it was given the status of International Biosphere Reserve and also became a World Heritage Site.

International Biosphere Reserves are part of a United Nations Educational, Scientific and Cultural Organisation (UNESCO) programme set up to protect a range of major ecosystems against which human impact can be measured. There are now 190 reserves across 50 countries, including the Everglades, an example of wetland biodiversity.

World Heritage Sites are also chosen by UNESCO as important cultural and heritage areas. The Everglades has been settled by humans for over 2000 years. It currently provides homes for 36 endangered or threatened wildlife species, e.g. the American alligator and crocodile, the Florida panther, the West Indian Manatee and the Cape Sable sparrow.

3 PEOPLE AND CITIES

Population patterns and structure

▶ Where do people live in the USA?

With an estimated population of 263 million in 1995, the USA is the third most highly populated country in the world. However, because of the size and variety of physical environments found in the USA, many of them quite harsh and unsuitable for human settlement, overall population density is only 28 per km². The pattern is one of extremes – densely populated urban areas contrasting with sparsely populated deserts, mountains and plains.

Seventy-six per cent of the population of the USA live in cities. Although this figure is fairly high, it is substantially lower than for other more economically developed countries (MEDCs). Life in the cities is quite different from life in rural areas, and many people move to urban areas in search of work or for what they see as a better quality of life (see pages 38–39).

State	Density	State	Density
Alabama	31	Montana	1.9
Alaska	0.4	Nebraska	8.1
Arizona	12.4	Nevada	4.2
Arkansas	17.4	N. Hampshire	47.5
California	73.4	N. Jersey	400
Colorado	12.4	N. Mexico	4.6
Connecticut	261	New York	147
Delaware	133	N. Carolina	52.5
Florida	92.3	N. Dakota	3.5
Georgia	43.2	Ohio	102
Hawaii	66.4	Oklahoma	17.8
Idaho	4.6	Oregon	11.6
Illinois	79.2	Pennsylvania	10
Indiana	59.5	Rhode Island	367
Iowa	19.3	S. Carolina	44.4
Kansas	11.6	S. Dakota	3.5
Kentucky	36	Tennnesee	45.9
Louisiana	36.7	Texas	25.1
Maine	15.4	Utah	8.1
Maryland	188	Vermont	23.6
Massachusetts	297	Virginia	60.2
Michigan	62.9	Washington	28.2
Minnesota	21.2	W.Virginia	28.6
Mississippi	20.8	Wisconsin	34.7
Missouri	28.6	Wyoming	1.9

A Population density by state (density per square km)

B Wide open spaces, the South Dakota Badlands

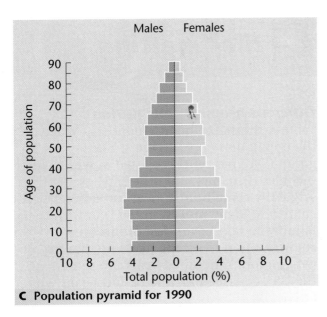

C Population pyramid for 1990

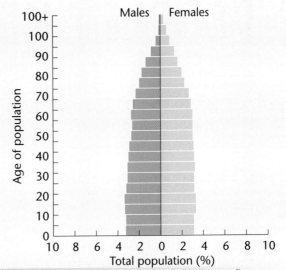

D Population pyramid for 2050 (estimated)

Population structure

As in many economically developed countries, the overall growth rate of the population in the USA is slowing down. Between 1950 and 1960 the increase was 1.7 per cent, falling to 0.9 per cent between 1980 and 1990. Although death rates have remained static (9 per 1000) since 1950, birth rates have fallen from 24 to 15 per 1000. This decline, coupled with one of the world's highest life expectancy rates, has led to a population structure showing a decrease in the proportion of children and an increase in young adults and the elderly (see graphs). The warm climate of southern states such as Florida, California and Arizona has attracted many retired people, but a high proportion of elderly people can put extra pressure on medical and other care services.

E Crowded city – Canal Street, New York City

FACT FILE

USA % population increase 1900–1990

1900–1920	39.3
1920–1940	24.6
1940–1960	37.1
1960–1980	26.1
1980–1990	9.2

Top ten US cities population (millions)

New York	7.3
Los Angeles	3.4
Chicago	2.7
Houston	1.7
Philadelphia	1.5
San Diego	1.2
Phoenix	1.0
Dallas	1.0
San Antonio	0.9
Detroit	0.9
(figures for cities, not metropolitan areas)	

A multicultural country – the 'melting pot'

▶ What is the composition of the USA's population today?

Only two million (0.8 per cent) of the USA's population of over 263 million (in 1998) are descendants of the native peoples of the country. There are over 500 different groups including the Inuit of Alaska and Native American tribes, many now living in reservations in the south west or north west of the USA. All other Americans are immigrants, or the descendants of immigrants.

Ethnic composition of the USA (1991) From Census data 1990	Million	%
Whites	199.69	79.2
Hispanics	22.35	
African American	29.99	11.9
Asian	10.51	4.2
Asian/Pacific Islanders	7.27	
Chinese	0.8	
Filipino	0.77	
Japanese	0.7	
Asian Indian	0.36	
Korean	0.35	
Vietnamese	0.26	
Native American	1.96	0.8
Others	9.8	3.9
Total	**251.9**	

A The USA's population by ethnic origin

Different peoples – one nation

Table **A** shows the main groups that make up the population (1991 figures). The biggest group (79.2 per cent) is classed as white, and includes Hispanics and others, whose families originally came from a great variety of other countries. Many moved to the USA with their families to take advantage of this 'new' country, often to escape hardship, poverty or persecution. A hundred years ago settlers in the USA consisted mainly of Europeans who arrived on the east coast, many settling in the north east. At the same time Asians and Europeans landed along the west coast.

During the first ten years of the twentieth century nearly nine million people moved to the USA. More recently Hispanics (Spanish speakers) have become the largest immigrant group, accounting for about 8.9 per cent of the USA's population. Many of these are immigrants from Mexico, Puerto Rico and Cuba. There are also thousands more who are not on the official census and have moved illegally across the border between the USA and Mexico (see pages 32–33). This wide-scale movement of different peoples to the USA earned it the name 'the melting pot'. It was a place where many different cultures met and lived together to form today's distinctive American culture and society. Today, many groups try to retain their own cultures and traditions as well.

B A New York classroom – typical of the diverse US population

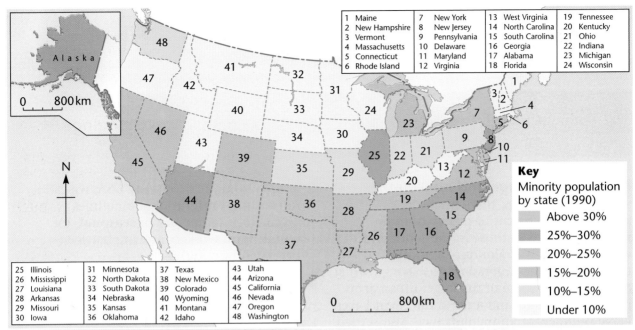

C The distribution of minority groups in the USA

Of the non-white population, African Americans are the largest group (11.9 per cent), with Asians forming 4.2 per cent. Many minority ethnic groups tend to live close together, often in urban, inner-city areas. Some of these areas have become well known throughout the world – for example San Francisco's Chinatown area with its Chinese shops and restaurants. However, racism and inequality can sometimes lead to tension, for example the Los Angeles riots of 1995. Rural areas have a far higher proportion of whites, although the states of the 'deep south' have had a large African-American population since the days of slavery.

The south east of the country has the highest proportion of African Americans, ranging from 25 to 35 per cent in Mississippi, Louisiana, Georgia, Alabama and North and South Carolina. The states of the south and south west have the highest proportion of Hispanics, with California and Texas (25 per cent) and New Mexico (30 per cent) being the highest.

	Washington DC	New York	Florida	Mississippi	Texas	California
Black	65.1%	14.3%	13.1%	35.4%	25.5%	25.8%
Hispanic	5.4%	12.2%	12.2%	0.6%	11.6%	7.0%
Asian	1.8%	3.7%	1.1%	0.5%	1.8%	9.1%
Native American	0.2%	0.3%	0.3%	0.3%	0.3%	0.6%

D Minorities in the capital and five selected states (1990)

FACT FILE

Origin of migrants to the USA, 1820 – 1990

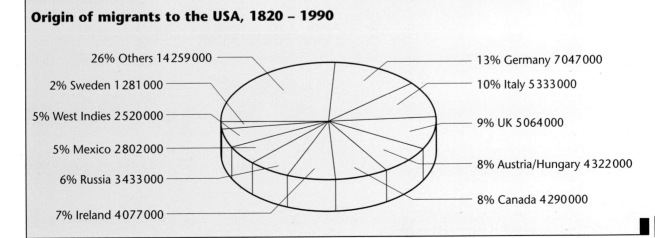

26% Others 14 259 000
2% Sweden 1 281 000
5% West Indies 2 520 000
5% Mexico 2 802 000
6% Russia 3 433 000
7% Ireland 4 077 000

13% Germany 7 047 000
10% Italy 5 333 000
9% UK 5 064 000
8% Austria/Hungary 4 322 000
8% Canada 4 290 000

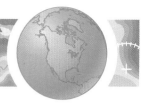

On the move

Population change and migration

Since the mid 1970s, there has been a significant movement of people from the north-east states to those in the south and west. States such as Florida, California and those around the Colorado river have grown at the expense of some of the larger urban areas in New York State, and around the Great Lakes. Large numbers of immigrants have also settled in the south west (map A).

Migration

When people move from place to place we call it **migration**. In a country as large as the USA migration is common. People often migrate when trying to find work or improve their quality of life. Movement within one country is called **internal migration**. It may be from a rural area to an urban one or a move out of an urban area to a quieter area; it could be local or from one state to another, for example from the north east to the south west. When movement is from one country to another, for example from Mexico to the USA, we call it **international migration**. Sometimes movement is temporary or **seasonal**, for example farm workers moving between Arizona and California.

B Reasons for moving

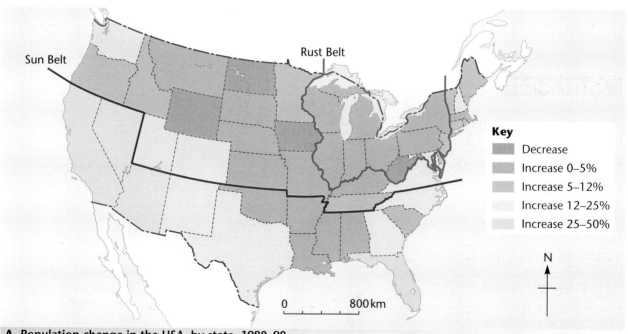

A Population change in the USA, by state, 1980–90

Large cities such as Los Angeles continue to attract newcomers in search of work (**urbanization**). Other people are moving away from cities, however. This movement is called **counter-urbanization**, and is generally caused by people who can afford to move and who leave the inner cities to improve their quality of life. Many are moving to rural areas or into new areas developing as the 'edge cities' outside Los Angeles and other big cities (see pages 38–39). Here they hope to find a cleaner environment, more space and less traffic.

By far the biggest internal migration in the USA is from the area known as the **Rust Belt**, in the north east of the country, to the southern states, often called the **Sun Belt** (see map **A**). The 'Rust Belt' states are so called because of the decline of the heavy industry that led to the area's success in the mid-twentieth century. Although modernization is beginning to take place, factories have been closing, forcing thousands of people to migrate to the south west for work. The landscape, climate and availability of land in the south west have attracted new high-tech and service industries, and people have been keen to move to a better quality of life and employment opportunities. Those migrating across the USA have been joined by **immigrants** to the USA, especially Mexico (see pages 32–33) and the countries of south-east Asia.

Geographers often try to explain the migration of people by looking at 'push' or 'pull' factors. If someone moves away from an area because they feel there is little there for them, we call this a **push** factor. If they move to another area because it seems very attractive to them, we call this a **pull** factor (**B**). Sometimes people migrate by choice (voluntary migration) – but some are forced into moving.

C An old derelict inner-city area of Philadelphia in the Rust Belt

D A spacious residential area out of the city

FACT FILE

Migration

Immigration: The movement of people into a country from another country.

Emigration: The movement of people out of one country from another country.

Most people choose to move from one country to another – this is called voluntary migration. Many move to seek jobs, money and a better quality of life. Others have little or no choice and may have to leave a country – this is called forced migration. This may be because of religious or political persecution or, more commonly, warfare. When people are forced to flee from their homes and arrive in another country they are known as refugees. Coping with large numbers of refugees can cause many problems for the recipient country. Many countries have introduced strict laws and quotas to deal with immigrants and refugees.

▶ Why do so many Mexicans migrate to the USA?

California, Arizona, New Mexico and Texas share their southern borders with Mexico – a total distance of over 2000km. In recent years the numbers of legal and illegal immigrants from Mexico have increased dramatically. The 1990 US census shows that over twelve million Mexicans live in the USA – but the actual figure is much higher, with perhaps another four or five million living there illegally. In 1995 over 800 000 people were caught and sent back to Mexico.

Why migrate?

Early migration was both encouraged and legal. In the 1960s many Mexican workers moved to the USA's southern states, especially to work in lower-paid jobs on farms, in factories or as cleaners and maids. US workers didn't want these types of jobs, and there were lots of them as the southern states grew rapidly. The Mexicans were usually seen as temporary or 'guest' migrant workers, sometimes working on a seasonal basis harvesting crops, sometimes for a few years.

Most of those who moved were seeking a better quality of life for themselves and their families. While some looked for the 'American Dream' – a well-paid job, a house, car and a good lifestyle, many were just looking for better conditions than those at home and a steady wage. In reality wages were low and many had to live in poor conditions, but they were still able to earn far more than in Mexico. Wages in Mexico are often ten times lower than those in the USA and unemployment is over 40 per cent in some areas.

Illegal immigration

During the 1970s and 80s many countries suffered from economic recession, the USA among them. Jobs were very difficult to find and many Americans in the southern states resented the Mexican immigrants, seeing them as a threat to their own quality of life. Like many minority groups in the USA, the Mexicans have developed their own shops, restaurants and culture. Many Americans welcome these different cultures, while for others they are a cause of resentment. Yet discrimination has not deterred would-be migrants. Despite the likelihood of being stopped by border guards, hundreds try to cross illegally every week, usually at night. It is estimated that up to a quarter of a million people move across the border each year.

A The Mexican/US border

	USA	Mexico
GNP per head	$26 980	$3 320
Life expectancy	73(M) 80(F)	67(M) 74(F)
Unemployment rate	5.6%	28%
Infant mortality rate (per 1000)	7	24
Birth rate (per 1000)	15	26
Adult literacy	99%	87%

B Comparisons between the USA and Mexico

Migration has a great effect on the areas people leave as well as on the areas they move to. One of the main problems is that it is usually younger people who migrate in search of work. The areas they leave behind are left with mainly older, retired inhabitants and children.

C The Mexican/US border

The Sanchez family – Luis and Ella, four children

'Now our eldest son is 19, he wants to move to the States. He says there is no future for him here. We don't want him to go – we need him to work for us – but he wants to make his own life. He thinks that once he goes to the States he will have money, a car, a house; but it won't happen. He'll end up with a poor job and we won't see him again.'

Jo Gomez (23 years) – migrant farm worker from Mexico

'I've been working as a vegetable picker near Phoenix for three years. The hours are very long - we start at 6 am and don't finish until 7 or 8 pm. But there is always work, whereas at home there is none. I miss my family and friends but I can't see myself going back. Maybe one day I will move to LA and find better work there.'

The Miller family – Gary and Linda, Marie (15 years) and Tommy (9 years)

'We moved to California when we got married 20 years ago. There were lots of opportunities and jobs were easy to get. Since then more and more people have moved here, mainly from Mexico. Most people speak Spanish, not English, and our neighbourhood seems more like Mexico than the USA. There are few well-paid jobs any more.'

D Reasons for moving to, and staying in, the USA

FACT FILE

Social data for Mexico and USA

Data		Mexico	USA
GNP per capita (in $)		3750	24750
Life expectancy (years)		67(M) 74(F)	73 (M) 80 (F)
Population density (per km^2)		49	28
Population structure (years\%)		0–14: 37	0–14: 21
		15–64: 57	15–64: 62
		65+: 6	65+: 17
Population growth rate (per 1000)		11	5
Infant mortality (per 1000)		36	8
Fertility rate		3	2
Population per doctor		621	420
Adult literacy (%)		87	99
Employment structure (%)	Primary:	23	3
	Secondary:	29	25
	Tertiary:	48	72

Los Angeles (1) Growth and development

▶ How has Los Angeles grown and developed?

TIMELINE

1769	Spanish missions set up along the Californian coast. Local Native Americans rounded up – many die.
1781	First real settlement – the Spanish build the 'Pueblo of Los Angeles' (where Downtown LA is today).
1800	LA's population is over 300, plus over 12 000 cattle – a 'cow town'.
1822	Mexico declares independence from Spain – Spanish mission system in California breaks down.
1850	Following takeover by the USA and a short war, California becomes an American state and LA becomes a city.
1868	The railway reaches LA from the east, bringing thousands of immigrants.
1888	LA actively campaigns to attract new immigrants, particularly from the American Midwest. Thousands come, especially farmers.
1899–1914	New port/harbour built.
1900	Oil discovered in LA, leading to a twenty-year boom.
1910	The film/movie industry begins in Hollywood, LA.
1913	Guaranteed water supply via the Owens valley aqueduct.
1920	Population doubles. LA becomes the financial centre of the West Coast. Many new civic buildings built.
1930	Great Depression. Many poorer (mainly unskilled) migrants move to LA from Texas, Oklahoma and Mexico.
1932	Olympic Games in new Coliseum stadium.
1933	Major earthquake.
1939	First freeway built.
1941	USA enters the Second World War. LA economy booms as aircraft/military supply industry grows. Many African Americans migrate here for work.
1950–70	Extensive freeway building throughout the region.
1955	Disneyland opens (first major theme park).
1965	Watts riots in South Central LA – 34 die. Rise of gangs.
1973	LA's first African-American mayor elected.
1984	Olympic Games.
1992	58 killed in USA's worst ever urban riots following the acquittal of police officers in the Rodney King beating case.
1994	Northridge earthquake kills 57 and causes over $25 billion damage.

A A high-altitude view of Los Angeles

Location

Los Angeles is on the Pacific coast of south-west California. The Los Angeles–Long Beach metropolitan area covers 1166km². With a population of over 14.5 million, it is the USA's second largest urban area. It is growing rapidly as migrants from within and outside the USA continue to move in.

Hazards and attractions

People have always been attracted to Los Angeles. The area has a warm Mediterranean climate and spectacular coastal and mountain scenery. From its early days as a cattle town, through to the beginnings of the film industry and the development of aerospace and electronics, thousands have moved here in search of work and the bright lights. Everyone in LA appears to be on the move – while many (especially from overseas) continue to move in, others have begun to move out to cities on the edge of the area, or away altogether. The city itself, with no real centre and miles of **freeways** (motorways), is dominated by, and built for, the car. This leads to choking air pollution and the famous LA **smogs**. LA has its natural hazards too. Built at the southern end

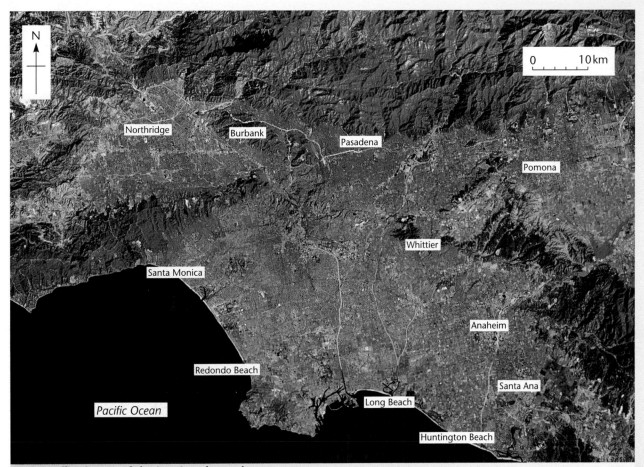

B A satellite image of the Los Angeles region

of the San Andreas fault, earthquakes are always a threat. In recent years forest fires and mudslides have also caused a lot of damage.

Economy

The success of LA's economy has varied through-out the twentieth century. Job opportunities have been the major pull factor for those moving here.

Although the 1990s have seen a rise in unemployment as the military and aerospace industries have declined, LA has a diverse enough economy not to be too badly affected. Major industries include media and entertainment; electronics and computers; medical instruments and clothing manufacture. LA is also an important tourist and financial centre and port, and has thousands of small businesses.

FACT FILE

Hollywood

Hollywood is located in the north west of Los Angeles. American movie makers moved there in 1911, mainly from New York. Hollywood enjoys long hours of sunshine, a great help to film making outdoors. It also had less strict laws to control the industry.

The area grew quickly as film companies relocated here and the great studio system began. By the 1920s, Paramount, MGM and Universal Studios were run by top directors such as Louis B. Mayer and Samuel Goldwyn, who had all become famous names in the film industry.

By the 1930s the studio system controlled not just film making, but writers, actors and directors. Hundreds of films were made. After the war competition from television and an unwillingness among actors to be contracted to just one employer, led to the decline of the great studios.

Today the industry has recovered a little, especially with the making of great adventure or blockbuster movies – by studios like 20th Century Fox now owned by media tycoon Rupert Murdoch. Thousands of hopefuls still move to LA each year in search of the Hollywood Dream.

Los Angeles (2) Traffic and transport

▶ **What are the problems of a 'car city'?**

The growth of freeways

More than any other urban area in the world, Los Angeles has developed and grown around the car. It had a tram service in the early part of the twentieth century, but by the 1930s the city was so congested that the first **freeway** was built in 1939. From the 1950s to the 1970s there was a massive freeway building programme. This encouraged the outward sprawl of Los Angeles and also helped widen the gap between rich and poor. Many of the new freeways cut through the poorer areas, avoiding the wealthier ones. Yet the wealthiest residents own most of the cars – the 20 per cent of the population with the highest income drive almost four times as many miles each year compared to the bottom 20 per cent of the population.

B A crowded freeway in LA

Air quality

For many years LA has been famous for its **smogs**, which occur on up to 300 days a year. Smog is a mixture of fog and smoke particles – 80 per cent of LA's smog is caused by emissions from motor vehicles. The geography of the area is also a factor. Cool air blows from the Pacific Ocean bringing fog inland, especially between May and October. This undercuts the warm air on the land, trapping fumes from cars and industry (see diagram **D**). The resulting smog causes major health problems for people with respiratory difficulties.

LA now has the strictest air quality standards in the USA. This has resulted in the best air quality for 40 years. The Environmental Protection Agency (EPA) is now campaigning for even tougher controls. If new recommendations are to be met, by 2010, 50 per cent of new cars will need to be 'zero emission' vehicles and 25 per cent will need to use cleaner fuels, for example gas.

The dominance of the car

Vast areas of LA are covered by freeways and roads connecting far-flung residential areas. Similarly, large areas are covered by car parks, car showrooms, car washes and repair

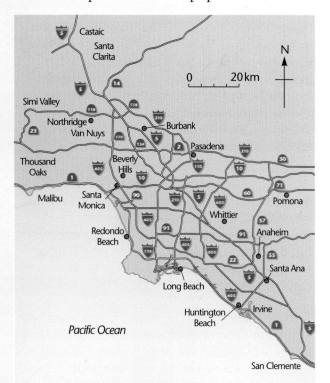

A LA's Freeways

workshops. Space is beginning to run out and traffic congestion and journey times are increasing. Half of California's taxes are spent on building and maintaining roads and on the Highway Patrol.

The way ahead?

For many years there was little real development of LA's public transport system, although the bus services are quite good. On average, LA residents make just over 50 trips per year on public transport. (In Zurich the figure is 500.) After years of argument a massive government-funded rail system is now underway. The MTA (Metropolitan Transit Authority) is developing three subway (underground) lines and an overground commuter rail service serving outlying areas (see map C). A proportion of the sales tax in LA is going towards funding these.

But for the car culture of LA to change significantly, a major change in attitude is needed. This may be essential if LA is to meet the stricter air quality standards planned for the twenty-first century. People need to be encouraged to move from the roads to the railways. Efficiency and cost are the keys to change.

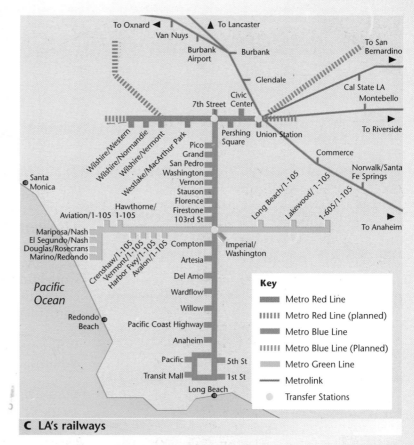

C LA's railways

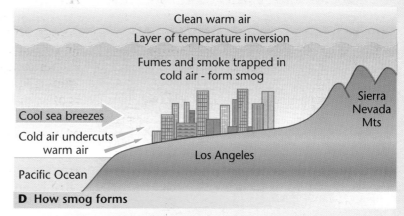

D How smog forms

FACT FILE

Metrolink – Southern California's commuter rail system

Metrolink is the regional commuter rail system for Los Angeles and southern California. Formed in 1991, it is responsible for just over 640km of railway.

Number of routes	6	Average daily passengers	26 642
Route names	San Bernadino, Ventura County, Santa Clarita/Antelope Valley, Riverside, Orange County, Inland Empire	Average commuter journey	58km
		Average speed	72km/h
Route km	669	% who used to drive	70%
Stations	46	% peak hour traffic cut	8.5%
Average no. of trains daily	106	No. of daily car trips removed	18 649

▶ How does the quality of life vary in Los Angeles?

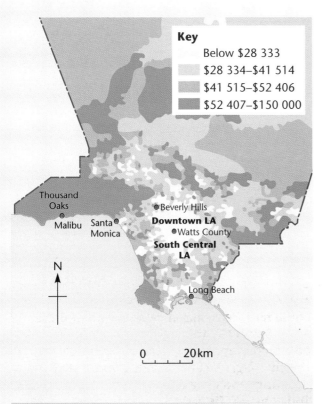

Key
- Below $28 333
- $28 334–$41 514
- $41 515–$52 406
- $52 407–$150 000

Thousand Oaks
Malibu Santa Monica
Beverly Hills
Downtown LA
Watts County
South Central LA
Long Beach

N

0   20 km

A Economic divisions in LA by income (1990)

Los Angeles is an example of a city with a dispersed pattern of land use (see page 35). The city grew up from 40 smaller centres, each of which had its own retail, business and industrial areas. The transport network has an important influence on economic activity and land use, with retail and industrial parks often located at freeway intersections. Although Los Angeles has a **downtown** area or **central business district** of high-rise office buildings, it is not so dominant as in other US cities.

Los Angeles is a very wealthy city, yet like many major urban areas around the world there are great inequalities in people's quality of life there. As in other US cities, there are wealthy and poor neighbourhoods, as well as areas where people from different ethnic groups live.

Generally the poorest are found closest to downtown, in areas such as South Central LA and Watts, or are close to some of the main freeways. The most affluent areas, for example Beverly Hills and Malibu, are in attractive suburban locations.

Migrants

Los Angeles has always been a multiracial city, as people have migrated there in search of work and a better life. But it is also a segregated city, with ethnic groups concentrated in particular areas.

White people live mainly in the more affluent suburbs.

Most African Americans moved here in the 1940s as LA developed as the centre of the USA's aircraft industry. Many settled in South Central LA, though today others live in wealthier suburbs.

Today over a third of the population is Hispanic, a figure which is growing. Mexican migrants have arrived in LA since it first began as a Spanish settlement; today it is the largest Mexican city outside Mexico. Others have come to escape wars in El Salvador and Nicaragua. Many Hispanic migrants move first to downtown or Broadway, though more now live in South Central LA.

Ethnic group	Population (thousands)
White*	9 403
Black	1 226
Native American	87
Asian	1 339
Others	2 473
Total	14 531

* Hispanic peoples make up about 33% of the white population

B The ethnic make up of LA

C Beverly Hills. This photo is typical of the vast mansions owned by some of the richest inhabitants of Los Angeles. Swimming pools, high walls, security gates and cameras are typical features of this area. The quality of life of those living here is amongst the highest in the country

D South Central LA. In contrast to Beverly Hills, some of LA's most disadvantaged people live in this downtown area where homelessness, poverty and crime are common place. Whilst many migrants arrive in this part of the city, if they can make some money they are quick to move away to improve their quality of life

LA's Asian population, which includes Koreans, Chinese and Japanese, has also grown rapidly in recent years. Many have achieved economic success through running small businesses and have then moved away from the centre.

Inequalities and perceptions

A study of Beverly Hills and South Central LA (see photos **C** and **D**) shows the vast differences in **quality of life** between wealthy and poor neighbourhoods. Many of the wealthier white population in areas like Beverly Hills are fearful of crime and have retreated into walled or gated residential estates with security guards. Yet the crime rate has fallen in recent years in these areas. South Central, near downtown, used to be a predominantly African-American part of the city. A gang culture grew up here, and shootings and drug dealing were commonplace. Today many Hispanics (called Latinos in LA) have moved in and created further tensions in the area. Many people are leaving to live in **edge cities** or outside LA, but, despite the problems, natural or man-made, thousands still migrate to LA every year.

FACT FILE

Spanish language in the USA
The first settlers to Los Angeles and the south west USA were the Spanish, many of whom where Catholic missionaries. Not surprisingly many settlements or places here are based on Spanish names and have religious connections:

Los Angeles = City of Angels
Las Vegas = fertile plains
San Francisco = Saint Francis
El Paso = the pass

Sierra = mountains
Colorado = coloured
Amarillo = yellow
Rio = river
Verde = green
Ciudad = city
Pueblo = people / town
Llana = flat land / plain
Mesa = table / plateau
Sacramento = the (holy) sacrements

4 ECONOMIC DEVELOPMENT

Industrial change and development

▶ **Where did industry in the USA begin?**
▶ **How has it changed?**

The USA is one of the world's leading industrial nations. At first farming was by far its most important industry, but from the 1850s onwards manufacturing industry developed rapidly. Much of this began and grew in the north east around the Great Lakes where there were raw materials such as iron and coal. Today over a quarter of the USA's manufacturing still takes place in the north east, whereas newer industries have located and developed rapidly in the south and south west.

The north east
Steel, car manufacturing and associated industries were at their peak between 1950 and 1970. The area then began to decline, and there were high levels of unemployment. Many Americans moved away to the south and west in search of a better quality of life. The north east became known as the **'Rust Belt'**. Today the outlook there is much better and the 'Big Three' US car companies (see page 44) are among those to have re-invested in the area. As the economic **recession** ended, run-down areas of cities such as Detroit have been renovated and improved.

	Primary (%)	Secondary (%)	Tertiary (%)
1970	8	32	60
1990	3	25	72

A Employment structure in the USA

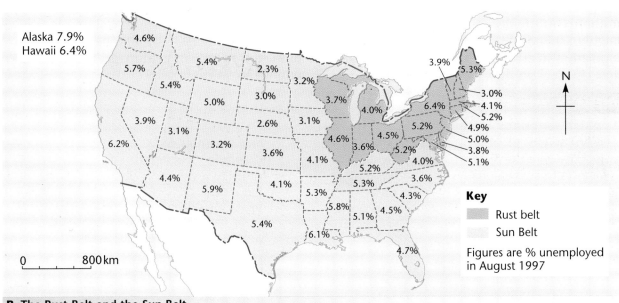

Alaska 7.9%
Hawaii 6.4%

Key
- Rust belt
- Sun Belt

Figures are % unemployed in August 1997

0 ⸻ 800 km

B The Rust Belt and the Sun Belt

40

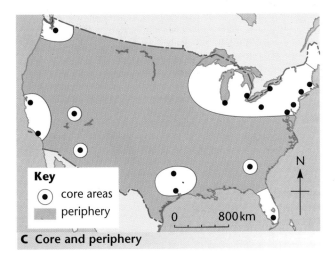

C Core and periphery

The move south

As the north east declined, the south boomed. **High-tech** industries producing electrical and computer goods use small components and, providing accessibility is good, they can locate almost anywhere. These are sometimes called **footloose** industries as they are not tied to a constant supply of heavy raw materials. It is easy to attract workers to live in the warm climate and attractive environment of the south, the USA's 'Sun Belt'. California's and Nevada's population has risen by over 25 per cent since 1980.

The climate, as well as the natural and purpose-built attractions of states such as California, Arizona and Florida attract millions of tourists each year, from both inside and outside the USA. Florida alone has almost 40 million visitors a year, enjoying sunny, beach-based holidays, the Everglades and other National Parks and theme parks such as Epcot and Disney World. As in many MEDCs, the highest proportion of the USA's workforce is employed in tertiary industries, many connected directly or indirectly with tourism.

Core and periphery

What has happened in the USA is a good example of what geographers refer to as the **core-periphery model**. The north east became the prosperous core of the country, producing wealth and attracting people towards it. Areas a long way from the core, on the **periphery** (edge), were usually much poorer. As the USA developed its industry, new **core** areas developed, for example around Los Angeles in California and Phoenix in Arizona. People moved away from the original core areas to new ones.

D Miami Beach – hotels and tourism form the major part of (tertiary) industry

1995	Primary	Secondary	Tertiary
Jobs in Florida	2%	9%	89%

E Types of employment in Florida

FACT FILE

Industrial pollution

As industry has developed, so has the problem of industrial pollution. Whether it be through discharges of chemical waste into rivers and lakes, or factory fumes into the atmosphere, industrialization in the US has led to widespread environmental damage.

One area of particular concern is the Great Lakes, on the northern border with Canada. Given the millions living along the shores of the Lakes and the amount of industry located here, it is not surprising that pollution has become a major problem. Amongst the causes are sewage discharge, waste products from the paper and steel industries, plus fertilisers washed from the farmland to the south. The quality of water supply for several states and the numbers of fish have been severely affected. New laws passed by both the US and Canadian governments have enforced stricter controls on both domestic and industrial waste disposal.

The rise of the industrial north east

▶ Why did industry in the USA first locate in the north east?
▶ Why did it decline?

As the USA began to develop its economy during the nineteenth century, it was the north east, around Pittsburgh, Cleveland, Detroit and Chicago, which became the centre of industry. There were many reasons for this (see table **A**), but the most important was the abundance of raw materials. As a result it was heavy industry which really took hold here – iron and steel, coal mining and engineering.

Iron and steel

Map **B** shows deposits of iron ore around Lake Superior and three large coalfields near Chicago and Pittsburgh. There were also areas of limestone used in the iron and steel-making process. The iron and steel industry provided work and money for the USA's growing population and economy, and supplied the steel for the railways and bridges which were opening up the west of the country.

Soon industries that *used* iron and steel followed, especially ship building and car manufacturing (see pages 44–45). The car industry was centred on Detroit (the birthplace

of Henry Ford, founder of the Ford Motor Company). Finished goods were sold in the USA or exported via the Great Lakes and the Atlantic coast.

A Why industry developed in the north east

Several major coalfields provided power for industry.

Availability of raw materials, e.g. iron ore, gave rise to a large number of iron and steel works.

Arrival of immigrant workers, often already skilled, to work in industry.

Accessibility. Despite cities such as Detroit being over 2000km inland, the Great Lakes were linked to the coast via the St Lawrence Seaway. As industry grew, access was improved to allow large ships to transport goods cheaply and easily for export.

Large, nearby home market and easily accessible overseas markets, e.g. Europe.

Agricultural produce from the northern and central states, e.g. wheat, was processed throughout the region and transported via the Great Lakes.

42 **B The industrial north east of the USA**

D Laser welding machine at a modern steel plant

C Heavy industry in the 1960s, Homestead, Pennsylvania

Decline

By the early 1970s US industry, and the north east in particular, began to decline. Other countries, for example Japan, Taiwan and South Korea, entered the world market for steel, producing it more cheaply than the USA. Iron ore deposits had been used up, and now had to be imported from abroad. The market for goods such as cars became more competitive, especially through Japanese car companies like Toyota. Factories in the north east were less modern, while wages and costs remained high.

Recovery

As industry declined, factories closed and parts of the north east became derelict. The area earned the name the 'Rust Belt'. People left to find work elsewhere, many migrating to the southern states.

The 1990s have been a time of recovery for the area. The car industry is thriving again as Ford, Chrysler and General Motors have modernized their factories. Run-down areas of Detroit have been redeveloped, unemployment has fallen and new companies and industries are beginning to move in.

BETHLEHEM STEEL CORPORATION

Bethlehem Steel, the second largest US steel producer, has had to change to survive the decline of the US steel industry in the 1970s. At its peak in 1957, it employed 165 000. It now employs 15 600. From the 1960s to the 1990s, it shut down or reduced production at many sites. However, it still produces 10 per cent of the USA's total amount of steel (10 million tonnes).

Today, its main production is at just three sites, the most important being Burns Harbor, which is 64km south east of Chicago. Here sheet steel and steel plate is produced in the USA's newest integrated steel works. It uses advanced computer technology throughout and employs 6000 workers.

FACT FILE

The changing fortunes of steel

Competition and a change in demand have led to great changes in the US steel industry during the 1980s and 90s. In 1970 the US imported just 13 per cent of its steel but by 1984 this had risen to 26 per cent and over 400 steel mills and related factories have been closed since 1980.

Over $50 billion was invested in the industry to modernize old factories and build new ones. As a result productivity has doubled since 1982, drastically cutting production costs and making the industry competitive again, despite a 30 per cent drop in the price. Once again the US is a major steel exporter. The 7 million tonne figure of 1995 has quadrupled the amount of steel sold abroad 10 years earlier. An increasing amount of scrap steel is now re-used in today's industry.

The changing car industry

How has the car industry developed – and changed ?

A brief history	
1903	Ford Motor Company founded, Detroit
1906	First cars exported
1913	Ford factories in Europe, Australia and Canada
1927	One million Model T Fords sold

Ford today (1997)	
Employees	364 000
Dealers	10 500 (worldwide)
Factories	in 31 countries/6 continents
Sales	$153 627 million (13% of world market)
Exports (1994)	120 133 vehicles
Other products	Construction machinery, industrial engines, glass and plastics
Second largest car/truck manufacturer in the world	
Second largest US company	
Second largest TNC (Transnational Company) in the world	

A The Ford Motor Company

At the beginning of the twentieth century, one of the USA's most successful manufacturing industries began. It was centred on Detroit in Michigan in the north east of the country. The area around Detroit soon became known as 'Motown' (Motor Town), as the car industry grew in size and importance.

Reasons for locating in the north east
Detroit became the centre of the industry in the USA because of:
- the availability of steel nearby
- the existence of other industries in the north east able to make and supply components
- a plentiful, skilled workforce
- a large local market for cars
- easy access to overseas markets
- its good, easily accessible location
- Henry Ford, the founder of the Ford Motor Company in 1903, who was from Michigan.

Boom and decline
From the early 1900s to the 1960s the industry boomed. The 'Big Three' US car companies – Ford, General Motors and Chrysler – all built factories here. Ford developed the assembly line method of production and for the first time cars could be produced cheaply and quickly in great numbers (see factfiles **A**). Workers were well paid and many people moved here, especially African Americans from the south of the country.

By the 1970s the boom had ended. Competition, especially from Japan, meant that it was often cheaper to import and buy foreign cars. Toyota overtook General Motors as the world's leading car production company. High wage rates in the USA were difficult to maintain as sales dropped and costs rose. Both the US car industry and the north east began to decline. Workers were laid off and older, less well equipped factories closed. People began to move away.

The car industry: 1980 to the present day
In the 1980s several new factories were built south of Detroit by Japanese car companies such as Toyota, Nissan and Honda. These were modern, state-of-the-art factories built on attractive **greenfield sites**, close to interstate highways (map **D**). They were encouraged by low taxes and rents as the area sought new jobs during the general economic recession of the time.

B Assembly line

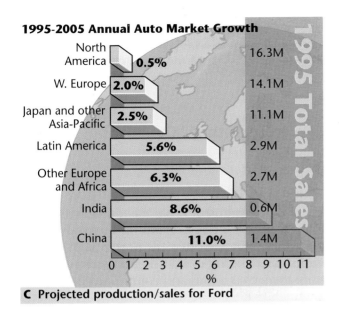

1995-2005 Annual Auto Market Growth

Region	Growth	1995 Total Sales
North America	0.5%	16.3M
W. Europe	2.0%	14.1M
Japan and other Asia-Pacific	2.5%	11.1M
Latin America	5.6%	2.9M
Other Europe and Africa	6.3%	2.7M
India	8.6%	0.6M
China	11.0%	1.4M

C Projected production/sales for Ford

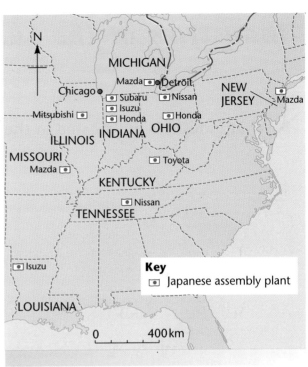

Key
◉ Japanese assembly plant

The future

Today Detroit itself is beginning to recover as a new generation of cars is developed. The 'Big Three' are co-operating with each other and the US government to develop more efficient, cleaner engines, share developments (and costs) in research and design and look at the new technology needed to produce a new generation of electric cars.

Since 1994 Ford has been developing its strategy for the year 2000 and beyond. It aims to create a single global management team, which increases efficiency and has created just five vehicle centres worldwide. The concept of a **global car** is a major change from the past when different models were built for different national markets. Research and Development (R&D) into new models is costly. If one new model can be found for a range of markets, the costs are more evenly spread and the company's products are more competitive. The CDW27 became Ford's first new global car. The same model is sold under different names – the Mondeo in Europe, the Middle East and Taiwan and the Contour or Mercury Mystique in North America.

FACT FILE

Henry Ford

Founder of the Ford Motor Company, Henry Ford was born on the family's farm in Dearborn, Michigan. At 16 he was an apprentice in Detroit before becoming an engineer. In 1893 he built his first car.

The Ford Motor Company was started in 1903. His company was the first to mass produce cars via the assembly line principle, including the famous 'Model T' in 1908 (15 million sold). To offset the tedious nature of assembly line work he doubled the pay of his workers – and greatly increased his company's profits.

By 1917 Ford was also producing trucks and tractors. In 1925 the first Ford Tri-star aircraft were built for the USA's first commercial airlines. During World War II car production halted, and Ford made aircraft engines, tanks and Jeeps.

In 1936 Henry Ford began the Ford Foundation for 'scientific, educational and charitable purposes'. Over $9 billion has since been allocated to a range of projects supporting equal opportunities, employment and protecting the environment. Henry Ford retired in 1945 and died in April 1947 leaving behind a successful transnational company and a great personal fortune.

Industries of the Sun Belt: California

▶ What industries are located in the south west of the USA? Why?

Key
----- State Boundary
—·— International Boundary
—— Motorway
✈ Airport
▨ Land above 1000m
▨ Land below 1000m

OREGON
IDAHO
Sierra Nevada (mt range)
Sacramento
NEVADA
San Francisco
San Jose
ARIZONA
Silicon Valley
CALIFORNIA
Pacific Ocean
N
Los Angeles ✈
San Diego
MEXICO
0   100km

A California

High–tech industry

The types of industries that have developed here in recent years are not reliant on bulky raw materials. They are often the newer, high-tech industries working in information technology, aerospace, electronics and communications. Companies are encouraged to locate here by the availability of cheaper land, with space to expand. Accessibility is good, with fast highways linking it with the rest of the USA and many international airports for overseas markets. Financial incentives, for example low taxes and wages compared with the north and east, have also helped persuade companies to move here.

Natural attractions include a warm, sunny climate and beautiful coastal and mountain scenery. By locating in new areas that have a pleasant environment, workers are attracted to jobs that also offer them a better quality of life. Migrants from across the USA are joined by those from south of the border, especially from Mexico, Puerto Rico and Cuba.

While it was in the north east that industry first prospered in the USA (see pages 42–43), there is no doubt that it is the southern 'Sun Belt' states that are booming today. Of these, California on the USA's western Pacific coast is one of the fastest growing and wealthiest. The population of 30 million has grown by over 25 per cent since 1980, making it the most densely populated state outside the north and east of the country. This has been caused partly by the migration of people from the rest of the USA in search of work and a better quality of life, and partly by immigration (see pages 28–29).

B Rapid transport, ideal climate – location of a greenfield site in California

Other industry

Although the high-tech industries of places like Silicon Valley are important (see table **D**), California has many other industries. Farming is very important and a wide range of crops are grown, for example grapes, citrus fruits and salad vegetables in the hot, sunny irrigated fields and valleys of California. No other state produces as much farming produce. Tourism is also an important employer in the entertainment, transport and other service industries.

California today

The 1990s have brought some problems to this boom area. The high-tech aerospace industry has suffered a decline as defence cutbacks were made. More and more work is carried out by automated production lines using robot technology. Farming too has become increasingly high tech, with automated picking, sorting and packing. Jobs have also been lost as other areas and countries compete for customers for their high-tech goods. **Footloose** industries can set up almost anywhere, and companies will look for cheaper locations.

There are worries about the very high demands for water for irrigation, vital if crops are to grow in the hot climate of California. Current levels of use may prove to be unsustainable in the future.

C Silicon Valley

Location	San Jose/Santa Clara Valley, south of San Francisco
Accessibility	Highway 280, several international airports
Companies	Canon, Toshiba, IBM, Hewlett Packard
Products	USA's major producer of computers, micro-electronics, aerospace goods, technical and communications equipment
Employees	Over half a million

D Silicon Valley

FACT FILE

Mission city to microchips

Santa Clara, 70km south of San Francisco and 15km west of San Jose, today lies at the centre of California's Silicon Valley.

The first settlement was in 1777 when the Spanish founded the Mission Santa Clara. In the 1850s many newcomers, attracted by the Gold Rush of 1849, settled there and farmed the fertile land of the Santa Clara Valley. The town developed rapidly, its economy based on manufacturing, seed and fruit industries. Amongst its products were fine leather and a range of wooden products from doors to coffins!

By 1906 the town numbered 5000 people and was spreading into the adjacent farmland and orchards. In the 1950s the development of the silicon chip spawned a massive electronics industry and the whole character of the area changed, as the base of its economy base moved from agricultural products to high tech. By 1990 Santa Clara's population reached 93 000, in the centre of Silicon Valley.

Energy and the economy

Energy consumption

The USA uses almost a quarter of the world's total energy production every year – more than any other country. Although it is one of the world's top producers of oil, gas and coal, over half its oil has to be imported. Despite experiments with solar power and other renewable sources, almost 90 per cent of the USA's energy still comes from non-renewable fossil fuels.

Fossil fuels – oil, gas and coal

The USA's abundant energy resources provided the basis for its economic and industrial development. Coal provided the north east with power to develop its heavy industries, especially iron and steel manufacturing. Today over 50 per cent of the USA's electricity is generated in coal-fired power stations. Coal is found in three main areas of the USA – the famous Appalachian coalfield, from Alabama to Pennsylvania; in Illinois and Indiana; and in smaller, scattered deposits in the Rocky Mountains and the plains of Montana (see map **D**). The importance of the eastern coalfields is now declining, partly because the coal here has a high sulphur content that causes high levels of pollution, unlike coal found in the west. Several Clean Air and Mining Acts in the past 25 years have placed restrictions on the mining and use of coal.

The USA uses more oil and natural gas than any country in the world, and is also one of the leading producers (see table **A**). Oil was first discovered in Pennsylvania in the late 1800s. The main fields today are in the south and west, especially in Texas, and, increasing in importance, Alaska. Over 85 per cent of the USA's crude oil is refined for use as fuel. For many years gas, found with oil, was burned and not used, but since the 1950s there has been a great increase in its use, especially to produce electricity. Unable to keep up with

B An oil refinery in Baton Rouge, Louisiana

	USA	UK	Japan	India
Coal (million tonnes)	937	53	6.3	288
Oil (million tonnes)	384	130	—	37
Natural gas (thousand terajoules)	20 159	2680	91	708

A Energy production 1995

	Oil	Gas	Coal	Nuclear	HEP	Other
1970	44.4%	32.8%	18.5%	0.3%	4.1%	0%
1995	38.2%	24.5%	21.6%	8.0%	3.9%	3.7%

C US energy consumption

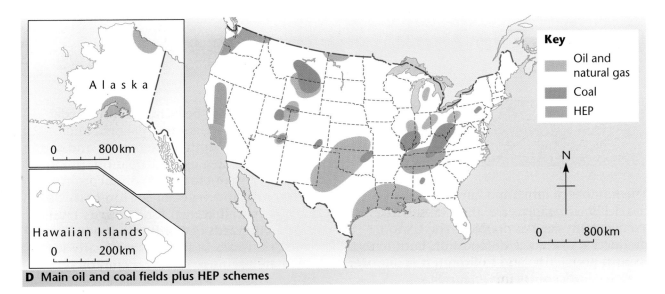

D Main oil and coal fields plus HEP schemes

Key: Oil and natural gas | Coal | HEP

demand from its own oilfields, the USA imports oil mainly from the Middle East, with gas from Canada and Mexico.

Other sources

There are over a hundred nuclear power stations in the USA which produce 8 per cent of the country's energy – 19 per cent of its total electricity generation. New stations are still in the planning stage as opposition to the nuclear industry has increased dramatically in recent years, following the accidents at Three Mile Island, Pennsylvania in 1979 and at Chernobyl in 1986. Strict legislation that is now in place and public opposition will make building future nuclear power stations very difficult.

Hydroelectric power stations are found along the Colorado, Tennessee and other major rivers. At present less than 1 per cent of energy is produced by renewable, clean 'alternative' sources such as wind, geothermal and solar power. While these may develop in favourable locations, for example solar power in California, it is unlikely that they will make a significant contribution to the USA's energy production in the near future.

FACT FILE

Three Mile Island

Opposition to nuclear power in countries like the USA has increased in recent years. This is partly because of a number of high profile accidents resulting in the leakage of radioactive gas. In 1979 the nuclear power station near Harrisburg in Pennsylvania suffered just such an accident. The pressurized water reactor (PWR) was shut down following a problem in the reactor, but human error in the control room led to the cooling system being shut down and the escape of a small quantity of radioactivity.

Although there was little risk to public health, the accident was very costly financially, and in terms of public confidence. Strict new laws were brought in, especially those regarding procedures in case of accidents, making it even more costly to construct new nuclear power reactors.

E Urban scene at night

Farming in the USA – agribusiness

▶ How is farming changing ?

The number of farms and farmers in the USA has declined rapidly since the 1950s, while average farm size has doubled. The USA produces a vast range of foodstuffs both to feed its own population and to export. It is one of the very few countries that is truly self-sufficient in terms of food. There are very few small farms. Farming is highly mechanized and organized – 'agribusiness' on a large scale.

The size and variety of soils and climates in the USA results in a wide variety of farming, whether crops or livestock. The central and north central states grow the most crops, especially cereals such as corn, wheat, barley and oats. Corn is by far the most important crop in the USA. The famous Corn Belt of Indiana, Illinois and Iowa stretches across the centre of the country before giving way to the vast wheat fields of the Prairies on the Great Plains of Dakota, Nebraska and Kansas. Tobacco is grown in Kentucky and South Carolina.

Cotton has always been important in the southern states – Georgia, Alabama and Mississippi. The hotter, drier south and south west, with massive use of irrigation, produce a great variety of crops including cotton, grapes, fruit, and vegetables. Florida is particularly well known for its **citrus fruits** and the vineyards of California produce some of the best wines in the world. Equally well known are the huge cattle ranches of Texas and Louisiana. Dairy farming is important in many states, especially Wisconsin, New York and Pennsylvania. Other livestock, especially pigs (or hogs as they are called in the USA) and sheep are reared in great numbers across the country.

Problems

With very **intensive farming** methods in use over huge areas of the country, problems have resulted. One of the most serious is the problem of soil erosion. Even small **fluctuations** in rainfall can lead to drought and the loss of topsoil through erosion. Most agricultural land is flat and exposed with few trees or hills to provide shelter from the wind which can simply blow the dry soil away. In the 1930s the drought was so bad that states

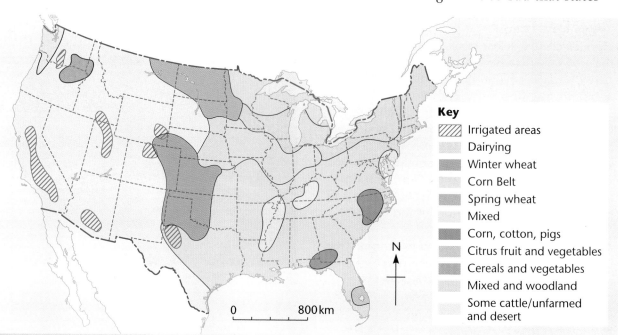

Key
- ▨ Irrigated areas
- Dairying
- Winter wheat
- Corn Belt
- Spring wheat
- Mixed
- Corn, cotton, pigs
- Citrus fruit and vegetables
- Cereals and vegetables
- Mixed and woodland
- Some cattle/unfarmed and desert

N

0   800 km

such as Oklahoma became known as the 'Dust Bowl'. Farms were abandoned as soil was blown away, crops failed and poverty spread throughout the region.

Many states, for example California and Arizona, rely on irrigation to grow their crops. Rivers such as the Colorado have been reduced to a trickle in places as water is removed to feed crops grown on what was once unproductive desert land. Many people worry how long this level of irrigation can last and whether this type of farming, using vast quantities of water and energy resources, is really sustainable in the future.

C Cattle ranching in Kansas

KANSAS

Once called the 'breadbasket' of the USA, the main industry in Kansas has traditionally been farming. As the pioneers and railroads pushed through from the east, the traditional landscape of grassland grazed by buffalo and inhabited by Native American tribes changed. Wheat and cattle took over and the Plains Indians were driven out.

From the middle of the nineteenth century until the droughts and recession of the 1930s, wheat farming and cattle ranching dominated the economy of the state. Today Kansas is the leading producer of wheat in the USA. Winter wheat is especially important, but other grain crops are also grown, for example rye, barley and oats. Six million cattle and other livestock are also important to the state's economy, bringing in over 60 per cent of the state's total earnings from agriculture.

B Kansas, showing extensive use of wheat fields – agribusiness

FACT FILE

Farming in California
California relies heavily on irrigation to grow its crops. Hot, sunny weather plus extensive artificial watering have led to the state becoming the leading agricultural producer and largest food processing state in the country. Its output is over 50 per cent greater than Texas, the next largest producer. It produces over half the USA's fruit and vegetables. Over 180 000 people are employed in processing a wide range of food and drink products.

% of total US crop	Crop produced in California
100	Olives, kiwifruit, pistachios, artichokes, almonds, dates
99	Raisins and walnuts
97	Grapes (table) and avocados
95	Brussel sprouts
93	Nectarines and tomatoes
91	Apricots
90	Broccoli
87	Plums
85	Wine and juice grapes
82	Lemon
81	Garlic
80	Strawberries
70–79	Honeydew melons, cauliflower, lettuce, celery
60–69	Cantaloupe melons, spinach, peaches, herbs
50–59	Pears and carrots

Trade and globalization

▶ Who are the USA's main trading partners?

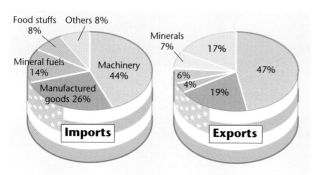

A The USA's imports and exports, 1991

	Imports from:	Exports to:
Canada	19.1%	21.9%
Mexico	9.7%	10.4%
Japan	13.8%	9.5%
Other Far East	16.6%	13.3%
Europe	19.2%	22.6%
Others	21.6%	22.4%

B The USA's trading partners, 1997

The USA is one of the world's most important trading nations. It buys (**imports**) and sells (**exports**) a wide variety of goods all over the world. The USA's main imports are machinery and equipment; manufactured goods, for example cars, clothing and computers; oil and gas and food products. The USA also exports many of these products, for example cars, food stuffs, machinery and minerals.

Measuring wealth

We often judge and compare the wealth of individual countries by measuring the **Gross Domestic Product** (GDP). This is the total value of products and services produced by a country per year; it is usually divided by the total population (per capita or person). The USA's GDP per capita today is ($24 750 in 1995) one of the highest in the world. The USA alone accounts for 10 per cent of the world's GDP.

The sheer size of the USA and its range of natural resources has much to do with its success as the world's largest economy. Almost three quarters of the USA's GDP is now generated by the service or tertiary sector.

Trade links and globalization

As a major global economy the USA trades across the world, but it has particularly close links with Canada, the Pacific Rim (Japan and the Far East) and the countries of western Europe. Trade with Canada and the Pacific Rim accounts for over half its imports and exports (see table **B**). In 1994 the USA joined with Canada and Mexico to form the **North American Free Trade Association** (NAFTA). This is a trading organization similar to the European Union, set up to help develop trade links between the three countries. One early benefit to the USA has been easier access to Mexico and its workforce. Many US companies have set up factories in Mexico to take advantage of much lower costs, for example wages and land. This contrasts with the number of Mexicans who have migrated to the USA for work. The nearness of the USA to Mexico and its markets is a great advantage.

C A container ship in San Francisco Bay

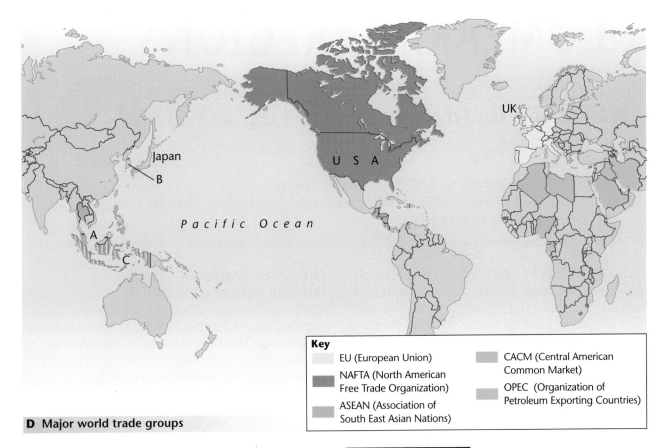

D Major world trade groups

Key
- EU (European Union)
- NAFTA (North American Free Trade Organization)
- ASEAN (Association of South East Asian Nations)
- CACM (Central American Common Market)
- OPEC (Organization of Petroleum Exporting Countries)

The future

Trade agreements between groups of countries are important and can help overcome difficulties such as import and export taxes. However, trade between the USA and Japan has often led to disagreements in recent years. For example, the USA has been unhappy that the sale of Japanese cars has caused the American car industry to decline. The USA has allowed **free trade**, while the Japanese have not always allowed free access to their own markets. Only in the last few years, for example, have the Japanese lifted strict rules on importing rice, partly through pressure from the USA who threatened their own import restrictions – a **trade war**.

Japan is just one of the countries in the Pacific Rim who have developed their economies rapidly during the twentieth century. They have a big impact on world trade and on the **globalization** of industry. Unfortunately such globalization can have both good and bad effects. In the late 1990s, Japan and the newer 'tiger' economies of South-East Asia suffered a major **recession**. Although the US economy remains strong, its trade ties with Japan are important. Japan's recession could therefore have a damaging effect on the USA.

FACT FILE

North American Free Trade Association
NAFTA is one of the world's newest and largest trading groups covering three countries with a combined population of over 360 million people. Over the past fifty years hundreds of thousands of Mexicans have moved (legally or illegally) to the USA for work. With the abolition of trade tariffs, many US companies have now built factories in Mexico.

This arrangement is mutually rewarding. The factories have to guarantee to employ a certain number of local workers and many of them are trained in specific skills. The money they earn then goes back into their own local and national economies. Also, a set proportion of raw materials have to be bought from Mexico. The US companies are given incentives to locate in Mexico, and pay lower wages than in the USA.

Alaska: wilderness versus wealth?

▶ **Should Alaska's oil reserves be developed further or should the wilderness be protected?**

Alaska is the USA's newest, largest, least densely populated and most remote state. Much of it is mountainous, and the climate is extreme (see table **B**). Almost a third of the state lies north of the Arctic Circle. Despite the difficult climate, it contains the greatest range of wildlife in the USA. It also contains the richest oil reserves. Uniquely, the majority of the land (70 per cent) is owned by the government.

Should Alaska seek to exploit and develop its vast oil resources and risk polluting a fragile environment, or should it protect its unique wilderness areas at any cost? As the oil companies battle to open new oil fields, environmentalists point to the disastrous effects of the USA's worst ever oil spill caused by the tanker *Exxon Valdez* in 1989 (see case study).

The Arctic National Wildlife Refuge (ANWR)

Many environmental groups are totally opposed to any further development of Alaska's oil reserves. They are alarmed at the possible destruction of this unique landscape. The *Exxon Valdez* spill reinforced their opposition. Organizations, such as the Northern Alaska Environment Centre (NAEC), have been working since 1971 to protect some of the USA's wildest and most pristine wilderness. One such area is the ANWR (see map **A**) in the north west of Alaska near Prudhoe Bay. Prudhoe Bay is the USA's largest oilfield, piping oil over 1000km south by overland pipeline to the port of Valdez. It was here that the *Exxon Valdez* took on its cargo as it set off for Los Angeles before running aground.

A Alaska

Key
- National park
- National forest
- National wildlife refuge

0 ———— 400km

N

Prudhoe Bay
Trans-Alaska pipeline
A N W R
Fairbanks
A L A S K A
U S A
C A N A D A
Bering Sea
Palmer
Anchorage
Valdez
Bristol Bay
Gulf of Alaska
Area affected by oil spill
Shelikof Strait

B Climate data for Fairbanks, Alaska

Month	Average temperature (°C)	Average precipitation (mm)
Jan	−18.6	14.4
Feb	−13.3	10.6
Mar	−4.4	9.1
Apr	5.7	6
May	15.5	14.4
June	21.6	34.5
July	22.5	44.2
Aug	19.1	44.2
Sept	12.5	26.1
Oct	2.0	2
Nov	−11.3	17.8
Dec	−17.2	18.7

C *Exxon Valdez* **oil spill – cleaning up on a beach in Alaska**

Oil companies are eager to develop oil reserves found in the ANWR. They claim that it can be done in an 'environmentally sensitive' way, citing Prudhoe Bay (smaller than the ANWR) as an example. Already 85 per cent of Alaska's budget comes from oil revenues, and each Alaskan receives about $1000 each year from these royalties. In 1979, a group called ASIA (Alaska Support Industry Alliance) claimed that not only would further development help the USA's future energy supplies, it would also create over 700 000 jobs across the USA. Its many leaflets and advertisements claim that the area is of little interest or use – 'the area is a flat, frozen wasteland for much of the year'. However, bills currently in the US Senate would prevent oil exploitation if passed.

Today, Alaska's dilemma – whether to exploit its resources for economic gain or protect and preserve the environment from such exploitation – is a common one throughout the world. As resources are used up, the pressure to develop known reserves in fragile ecosystems will increase.

ANWR today

Called America's 'Serengeti' (after the Tanzanian nature reserve in Africa), it is home to millions of migratory birds.

It is the USA's most important polar bear habitat.

Thousands of caribou live and breed here.

12 000 Gwich'in Native Americans live in the area.

Dangers from future oil development

Roads and pipelines would block the migration of wildlife.

Toxic waste would pollute wetlands and rivers killing fish and wildlife.

Noise from traffic and equipment would disturb wildlife. The area would no longer be a wilderness area.

The survival of the Native Americans' traditional way of life would be threatened.

D Arctic National Wildlife Reserve

THE EXXON VALDEZ DISASTER

Date	24 March 1989
Accident details	The tanker *Exxon Valdez* ran aground on Bligh Reef as it was leaving Valdez.
Cargo	1.2 million barrels of crude oil
Amount spilt	11.2 million gallons (50.8 million litres) (about 20% of the cargo)
Area affected	Islands in and around Prince William Sound; 1900km of coastline, three National Parks, four wildlife reserves
Oil spilt	40% of the oil deposited on beaches. 35% evaporated. 25% floated into the Gulf of Alaska.
Damage	Local fishing industry devastated. Thousands of birds and animals killed or poisoned including otters, deer, bears, eagles, salmon, etc. Water and beaches covered in oil and toxic fumes.
Costs	Clean-up operations cost Exxon $1 billion, plus a further $1 billion in compensation.

FACT FILE

Alaska

- Alaska belonged to the former USSR and was sold to the USA for $7 million in 1867.
- Mount McKinley (also known as Denali) is, at nearly 6500m, the highest mountain in North America.
- Alaska is sometimes called 'The Last Frontier' and 'Land of the Midnight Sun' and has large areas of wilderness and snow-covered mountains. In summer there are between 18 and 20 hours of sunlight every day.
- the main river, the Yukon, is one of North America's longest rivers (3185km), starting in Canada and flowing into the Bering Sea.
- earthquakes and volcanic activity are common – 8 of the 'top ten' biggest USA earthquakes have occurred here.
- the USA's largest two national forests are in Alaska – Chugach and Tongass.
- almost a third of the state lies north of the Arctic Circle.

Florida: the USA's 'Sunshine State'

▶ Why is Florida so attractive as a tourist and retirement destination?

Florida's location in the south west of the USA, just north of the Tropic of Cancer, gives it a warm, sub-tropical climate all year (see table **B**). Not surprisingly it is known as the 'Sunshine State', and it attracts millions of tourists annually. It is also the favourite retirement destination for many elderly Americans.

Florida has the highest proportion of people over 65 in any state in the USA – 18.5 per cent in 1996, compared to an average of 12.8 per cent across the USA. Many have moved to Florida to enjoy the warm, sunny weather. Immigration from outside the USA has also affected Florida's population, which has tripled since 1960. Only 23.8 per cent of the population is under 18, which is less than for all but two other states. With such a high number of retired residents, Florida's working population numbers just 58.8 per cent – one of the lowest proportions in the USA.

Month	Average temperature (°C)	Average precipitation (mm)
Jan	15	61
Feb	16	74
Mar	19	79
Apr	22	38
May	25	86
June	27	188
July	28	188
Aug	28	163
Sept	27	150
Oct	24	53
Nov	20	48
Dec	17	53

B Climate statistics, Orlando, Florida

Florida ranks highest in the USA for violent crime with a rate of over 1000 violent crimes per 100 000 population – almost twice the national average. However, this does not take into account the huge volume of visitors to the state who add considerably to the population. Although a few high-profile crimes have been widely reported, Florida remains the most popular holiday destination (outside Europe) for UK tourists.

Tourism

Florida's climate and scenery help attract over 20 million tourists each year. Florida boasts three National Parks including the Everglades (see pages 24–25). The Everglades alone attract almost ten million visitors each year. The most popular beach resorts include Miami, Clearwater, the Florida Keys and Fort Lauderdale. However, there is one disadvantage to Florida's favourable physical geography – it lies in the USA's hurricane area. While there are few deaths from these fierce tropical storms, thanks to advance radar warning, damage can still be extensive, as Hurricane Andrew showed in 1992 (see pages 16–17) and Hurricane Georges in 1998.

Florida

Disneyworld

Everglades

A unique environment of mangrove and other swamps, teeming with wildlife. Follow the boardwalk trails or take a boat ride to get close to nature!!

Sun, Sea and Sand

Hot, subtropical weather and stunning coastal landscapes make Florida and its many offshore islands the ideal resort for those in search of sun, sea and sand.

Children of *all* ages (including those over 18) will want to visit Disneyworld and its most famous resident, Mickey Mouse. Meet Mickey and his friends and enjoy great rides and entertainment.

C Holiday brochure

Not all of Florida's attractions are natural. They also include the Kennedy Space Centre and numerous theme and leisure parks, for example Disneyworld, the EPCOT Centre, Universal Studios and Sea World.

FACT FILE

Kennedy Space Center and Cape Canaveral
Located only one hour east of Orlando, on Florida's Atlantic coast, the Kennedy Space Center attracts nearly 4 million visitors per year. The Visitor Complex includes the outdoor Rocket Garden, the Astronauts' Memorial and the full-sized replica of the 'Explorer' Space Shuttle. Bus tours of the launch area also stop at the huge 52-storey Vehicle Assembly building, where the Space Shuttles are built.

Tours of nearby Cape Canaveral Air Force Station show where the US space program began, when the National Aeronautics and Space Administration (NASA) was set up in 1958. Existing rockets and launch pads at Cape Canaveral were adapted to launch early satellites and the Mercury and Gemini astronauts. There were more than 20 working launch pads during its most active period in the early 1960s, and satellites and automated spacecraft are still being launched from the Cape today. The re-useable Space Shuttles have made repeated trips into space since 'Columbia' made its first flight in 1981.

The area is bordered by the Canaveral National Seashore, and Merritt Island National Wildlife Refuge. The National Seashore is one of the last sections of undeveloped beach on the east coast of Florida; Merritt Island National Wildlife Refuge protects more endangered species of birds, mammals and reptiles than any other area of the US.

New York City and State

New York City is the third largest and one of the most famous cities in the world. New York State is one of the USA's original thirteen states. It stretches inland to the west as far as Niagara Falls (approximately 500km).

New York City

New York was first developed as a port and trading centre on the Hudson and East Rivers in the seventeenth century by the Dutch, and then by the British. The familiar cityscape of skyscrapers on New York's Manhattan Island today (see photo **A**) was built much later during the second half of the twentieth century. Over 20 million people, mainly from Europe, emigrated to the USA during the late nineteenth and early twentieth centuries. As the immigrants arrived to be 'processed' on Ellis Island, they were greeted by the nearby famous Statue of Liberty – built in 1886 as a symbol of freedom.

Today New York City has a population of 7.3 million, although the vast metropolitan area which has grown around it numbers 19.5 million. As with many USA cities it has a wide ethnic mix (see pie chart **B**). The city covers 800km^2 and it is divided into five counties – Queens, Brooklyn, Staten Island, Manhattan and the Bronx. Apart from the Bronx, which is part of the mainland, these counties occupy three of the many islands on New York's Atlantic coast.

The city is an important international trade and financial centre and contains the headquarters of the United Nations. Its many theatres, museums, galleries and arts centres attract visitors from both inside and outside the USA – tourism is an important part of its economy. It also has a large clothing industry.

New York shares with many large cities problems of traffic congestion, over-crowding and crime. New York was known as one of the most violent cities in the world, but there has been dramatic improvement in recent years, partly due to the police policy of 'zero tolerance'.

A New York skyline from the air

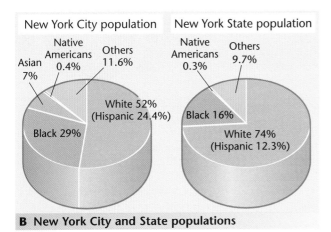

B New York City and State populations

New York City population — Native Americans 0.4%, Asian 7%, Others 11.6%, White 52% (Hispanic 24.4%), Black 29%

New York State population — Native Americans 0.3%, Others 9.7%, Black 16%, White 74% (Hispanic 12.3%)

New York State

The contrast between the busy urban environment of the city and the great variety of landscapes in the state is dramatic. Travelling north west from the city you first cross the Catskill mountains before turning west to the Finger Lakes. Beyond these, on the border with Canada, are the Niagara Falls (see factfile and photo **D**) and the Great Lakes. To the east lie the coastal landscapes and beaches of Long Island and the Atlantic seaboard.

With such a wide range of attractive landscapes (plus the lure of New York City), over 50 million visitors spend almost $20 billion in the state every year. While tourism is an important sector of the economy, primary industry – farming and forestry – is also important. There are over 35 000 farms, concentrating mainly on dairying, and 53 per cent of the state is forested; 70 per cent of the timber cut annually is hardwood. Secondary industry has declined in recent years.

C New York State

New York State is typical of the diverse physical and human geography of the USA, with its range of landscapes, uneven population distribution and rural/urban differences.

NIAGARA FALLS FACTFILE

Location	On Niagara River flowing north between Lake Erie and Lake Ontario.
Falls	Three waterfalls: American (182 feet drop); Horseshoe (176 feet) and Bridal Veil.
Volume	3.4 million litres per second (summer months)
Age	10 000–30 000 years
Visitors	Access to Falls by foot, boat or helicopter (50 000 honeymoon couples visit per year!)

D Niagara Falls

FACT FILE

New York City – the Big Apple
- the USA's biggest city and first capital
- named after the Duke of York (later James II) of England in 1664
- nicknamed the 'Big Apple' by jazz musicians in the 1930's who referred to any town or city as the 'apple' – New York was big time, therefore it became the 'Big Apple'!
- famous landmarks include the Empire State Building (381m) and the World Trade Centre (411m)
- the Statue of Liberty in New York Harbour was given to the USA by the French in 1886.

Statistics

	UK	CHINA	FRANCE	SOUTH AFRICA	USA
Area (km²)	244 880	9 596 960	551 500	1 221 040	9 809 431
Total population: (millions)	58.3	1210.0	58.8	44.0	263.6
Population density: (people per km²)	243	130	107	35	28

Population

	UK	CHINA	FRANCE	SOUTH AFRICA	USA
Birth rate (per 1000)	13	17	13	27	15
Death rate (per 1000)	11	7	9	12	9
Life expectancy (male and female)	74M 79F	69M 72F	75M 83F	54M 58F	73M 79F
Fertility: (children per female)	2	2	2	4	2
population structure (%): 0-14 16-59 60+	19 61 21	27 65 9	20 61 19	37 57 6	21 62 17
Urban population: (% of population)	90	29	74	57	77

Environment and economy

	UK	CHINA	FRANCE	SOUTH AFRICA	USA
Rate of urban population growth per year (%)	0.3	4.3	0.4	3.0	1.3
Land use (%): arable grass forest	27 46 10	10 43 14	33 20 27	10 67 4	19 25 30
workforce in (%): farming industry services	2 28 70	73 14 13	6 29 65	13 25 62	3 25 72
GNP per person (US$)	$18 700	$620	$24 990	$3 160	$24 750
Unemployment (%)	8.3	2.8	11.6	30	5.6
Energy used (tonnes/person/year)	5.4	0.35	5.43	2.49	10.74

Society and quality of life

	UK	CHINA	FRANCE	SOUTH AFRICA	USA
Infant mortality (death per 1000)	8	38	6	53	7
People per doctor	300	1000	333	1750	420
Food supply (calories per person per day)	3317	2727	3633	2695	3732
Adult literacy (%)	99	70	99	81	99
TVs per 1000 people	434	31	407	98	814
Aid received or given per person (US$)	$51 given	$3 received	$137 given	$10 received	$33 given
Education spending (% of GNP)	5.3	2.4	3.8	3.8	7.0
Military spending(% of GNP)	4.0	3.7	3.0	3.0	5.3
UN Human Development Index (out of 1.0)	0.92	0.59	0.93	0.71	0.94

Figures are for 1998–99. Source: *Philip's Geographical Digest* (United Nations, World Bank). The Human Development Index is worked out by the UN. It is a summary of national income, life expectancy, adult literacy and education. It is a measure of human progress. In 1992, the HDI ranged from 0.59 to 0.94 (China and USA).

Key statistics
Longest river: Mississippi-Missouri (6020km)
Highest mountain: Mount McKinley (6194m)
Largest lake: Lake Superior (82 071 km^2)
              (with Canada)
Largest city: New York (7.3M)
Capital: Washington DC
Languages: English, Spanish
Currency: Dollar
Religion(s): Protestant (53%);
             Roman Catholic (26%);
             other (21%)

Social
Population of largest cities:

New York	7 333 000
Los Angeles	3 448 000
Chicago	2 731 000
Houston	1 702 000
Philadelphia	1 524 000
San Diego	1 151 000

Economic
Imports and exports:

	Imports (%)	Exports (%)
Food and live animals	4.0	6.9
Beverages and tobacco	0.8	1.6
Crude materials (excl. fuels)	2.8	5.8
Minerals fuels, lubricants	8.7	1.8
Animals and vegetables oils and fats	0.0	0.3
Chemicals	5.1	10.0
Manufacturing goods	12.2	8.8
Machinery and transport equipment	45.6	49.2
Miscellaneous goods	17.2	11.0
Total US$M Main export market: Canada (22%) Main import source: Canada (19.8%)	689 030	512 337

Agricultural
Land use

Area:	9 573 000 km^2
Arable land:	19.4%
Permanent crops:	0.21%
Permanent grassland:	25%
Forest:	29.9%
Other:	25.5%
Irrigated land:	214 000 km^2

Miscellaneous:

Armed forces:	1 547 000
Political parties:	Democrats and Republicans
Death penalty:	Still in force
Defence spend:	3.8% of GDP
Education spend:	5.5% of GDP
Hospital beds:	1 per 230 people
TV sets:	805 per 1000 people
Radios:	2093 per 1000 people

agribusiness commercial farming carried out on a large scale, typically by transnational companies

capital intensive investing money to buy in technology / machinery to do work rather than using people

citrus fruits fruits such as oranges, grapefruits, lemons and limes

Central business district (CBD) area at the centre of towns and cities where most offices and shops are found - typically high rise buildings

continental mainland / inland, away from the sea

composite volcano a large volcano composed of many different layers of e.g. ash and lava, over a long period of time

conservative margin the boundary between two plates moving sideways past each other

core an area of concentrated economic activity and development

core-periphery model a model showing differences in the location of economic growth in a country. Growth is highest in the core region(s) and slower in the poorer, less developed periphery region(s)

counter-urbanization the movement of people away from urban areas to smaller more rural areas

downtown the central or lower part of a city, especially the commercial part

drip irrigation method of watering large plants e.g. fruit trees using small valves in pipelines which can be turned on or off, delivering a water supply to the base of each individual plant/tree

edge cities new cities being built and developed outside or on the edge of existing cities and urban areas

effusive gushing lava flowing out above ground to form surface rock

epicentre the point on the surface of the land directly above the centre (focus) of an earthquake / seismic activity

eutrophication when large amounts of nutrients (often nitrates from fertilisers) are present in water causing plants to grow rapidly, reducing the amount of oxygen in the water

exports goods sold abroad to other countries

faults lines of weakness or fractures in the earth's crust where earthquakes have occurred, displacing rock on one or both sides

field irrigation water crops by flooding an entire field with water and letting it drain away. Uses lots of water

footloose industries that are not tied to specific locations e.g. next to raw material source

flood irrigation water crops by flooding an entire field with water and letting it drain away. Uses lots of water

flood plain area of flat land next to a river, liable to flood

fluctuations changes from the normal, up or down

freeway USA motorway

free trade trading between countries without duties, barriers or subsidies

global car a car made for international markets - one model sold across the world, not different models for different countries

globalisation the trend for transnational companies to locate factories throughout the world to reduce costs and increase market share

greenfield sites areas of land, usually outside urban areas, not previously used for industry

Gross Domestic Product (GDP) a measure of a country's wealth calculated by assessing the value of products and services produced each year

high tech high technology e.g. use of ICT

immigrant someone who moves into a country from another one

imports buying goods or services from another country into your own

intensive farming using land, labour and capital to maximise production

interception plants/vegetation delaying rainfall from reaching the ground

internal migration movement of people from one place to another within a country

international migration movement of people from one country to another

levées embankments at the side of a river which help hold back flood water. They may be made artificially or naturally

maritime influenced by the sea, leading to a smaller annual temperature range

meanders natural bends in the channel/course of a river

migration the movement of people from place to place

North American Free Trade Association (NAFTA) a trading group comprising Canada, Mexico and the USA

periphery on the edge / away from the centre or core. Growth and economic development is usually slower here

plates large sections of the earth's crust which move around on the liquid rock below

push factor reasons for wanting to move away from a place

pull factor reasons for wanting to move to another place

quality of life how good or bad people feel about their way of life and the environment around them

recession a fall in economic prosperity, often temporary

run-off the movement of water off the surface of the land via e.g. a stream, river or after heavy rain

Rust Belt the name given to a group of north eastern states where industry declined in the 1970's and 80's

saturated full of water / waterlogged

seasonal migration the temporary movement of people at certain times of year e.g. farm workers in spring/summer to harvest crops

shield volcano a wide, gently sloping volcano made from thin, runny lava

smogs low level clouds causing poor visibility and breathing difficulties caused by the build up of traffic fumes and pollution

sprinkler irrigation watering large areas of lands using sprinklers or sprinkler booms

sub-tropical wetlands warm, wet areas just outside the Tropics where wetland plants and animals thrive

Sun Belt name given to the USA's southern (especially south western) states because of the warm climate

temperature range the difference between the highest average temperature and the lowest

transform fault where two plates are sliding laterally past each other in opposite directions

urbanisation the increase and growth of towns and urban areas

wing dykes concrete walls built out into a river to slow the current one side and speed it up the other, allowing a deep water channel to develop

Index

Bold type refers to terms included in the glossary *Italic* type refers to photographs or maps.

African Americans 11, 29, 38
air quality standards 36, 37
Alabama 29, 50
Alaska 5, 11, 28, 48, 54–5, *54*
Appalachian Mountains 5
Arctic Circle *5*, 54, 55
Arctic National Wildlife Refuge (ANWR) 54, 55
Arizona , 18, 20–1, 27, 30, 32, 41, 51

Bethlehem Steel Corporation 43
Beverly Hills 38, 39, *39*

California 18, 27, 29, 30, 32, 41, 46–7, *46*, *46*, 51
Californian Gold Rush 10
Cape Canaveral 57
car culture 36–7
car manufacturing 40, 42, 43, 44–5, *44*, 53
Carolinas 29, 50
Cascade mountains 8, 15
Central Plains 9
Chicago 42
Civil Rights movement 11
Cleveland 42
climate 5, 8–9, *8*, 54, 56
   climate zones *8*
coal 42, 48, *49*
Colorado river 18–19, *19*, 20, 30, 51
core-periphery model 41, *41*, 62
Corn Belt 50
counter-urbanization 31, 62
crime 39, 56, 58

dams 18, 19, 22
Detroit 40, 42, 43, 44, 45
Disneyworld 57
Dust Bowl 51

earthquakes 12–13, 35, 55
economy 60
edge cities 31, 39, 62
employment structure 40, 41
energy resources and consumption 48–9, 60
eutrophication 25, 62
Everglades National Park 24–5, *24*, *25*, 56, 57
Exxon Valdez oil spill 54, 55, *55*

farming 9, 18, 20, 21, 24, 42, 47, 50–1, *50*, 59, 60, 61
   agribusiness 50, 62
   capital--intensive farms 18, 62
   crops 21, 47, 50, 51
   intensive farming 50, 62
film industry 35
floods 19, 22–3
Florida 5, 16, 24–5, 27, 30, 41, 50, 56–7, *56*
Florida Keys 6, 7, *7*
Ford, Henry 42, 44, 45
Ford Motor Company 43, 44, 45
forests 9, 55, 59
fossil fuels 48
freeways 34, 36, *36*, 62
Georgia 29, 50
globalization 53, 62
Grand Canyon 6, 7, *7*, 18, 19
grasslands 9, 9
Great Lakes 30, 40, 41, 42
Great Plains 10
greenfield sites 44, *46*, 62
Gross Domestic Product (GDP) 52, 60, 62

Hawaii 5, 11, 14–15
Hispanics 28, 29, 38, 39
history of the USA 10–11

Hollywood 35
Hoover dam *18*, 19
Hurricane Andrew 16, *16*
hurricanes 16, 17, 56
hydroelectric power 18, 19, 49

immigrants 11, 28, 29, 30, 31, 32, 42, 46, 56, 58, 62
   illegal immigrants 28, 32, 53
imports and exports 52, 61, 62
industry 31, 40–7
   footloose industries 41, 47, 62
   high-tech industries 31, 41, 46, 47, 62
   industrial north east 40, 41, 42–3, *42*
International Biosphere Reserves 25
Inuit 28
iron and steel industries 40, 42, 43, *43*, 48
irrigation 18, *18*, 19, 20, 47, 51, 62, 63

Japan 44, 53

Kansas 50, 51, *51*
Kennedy Space Center 57
King, Dr Martin Luther 11
Kissimmee river 24

Lake Mead *18*, 19
language 39, 61
Las Vegas 18
Los Angeles 12, 13, *13*, *13*, 29, 31, 34–9, *34*, *35*, *36*, *39*, 41
   climate 9
   economic divisions 38, *38*
   economy 35
   ethnic groups 38–9
   freeways 34, 36, *36*
   growth and development 34–5
   traffic amd transport 34, 36–7
Louisiana 16, 29, 50

Mexican/US border 32, *32*, *33*
Mexico 32, 52, 53
Miami Beach *41*
migration 30–3, 38, 46, 63
   across the Mexican border 32–3
   forced migration 31
   internal migration 30, 31, 63
   international migration 30, 63
   seasonal migration 30, 63
   voluntary migration 31
Mississippi 29, 50
Mississippi river 22–3, *22*
Mount Kilauea 14, 15, *15*
Mount McKinley 55
Mount St Helens 14, *14*, 15
mountain ranges 5, 8
multicultural society 28–9

National Parks 6, 7, 24–5, 41
Native Americans 10, 11, *11*, 19, 20, 28
natural disasters 12–17, 35, 55, 56
natural gas 48
Nevada 18, 41
New Mexico 29, 32
New Orleans 9
New York City 5, 9, *27*, 58–9, *58*
New York State 30, 50, 59, *59*
Niagara Falls 6, 59, *59*
North American Free Trade Association (NAFTA) 52, 53, 63
nuclear power stations 49

oil 48–9, *48*, *49*, 54, 55

Philadelphia *31*
Phoenix 9, 18, 20–1, *21*, 41
physical features *4*, *5*
pioneers 10
Pittsburgh 42
pollution 24, 25, 34, 36, 41, 48
population 20, 26–31, 56, 58, 59, 60, 61
   density 26

ethnic composition 28–9, *29*
   growth 10, 11, 25, 27, 41, 46
   population change by state *30*
   structure 27
   top ten US cities 27
   see also migration
public transport 37

quality of life 38–9, 63

rainfall 8–9, 22, 25, 50
raw materials 42
recession 40, 44, 53, 63
refugees 31
reservoirs 18, 22
rivers 18–19
   levées 22, 23, 25, 63
   meanders 22, 63
   wing dykes 22, 63
Rocky Mountains 5, 6, 19, 48
Rust Belt 31, 40, *40*, 43, 63

San Andreas fault 12, 13, 35
San Francisco 13, 29
Santa Clara 47
sawgrass 24
ship building 42
Sierra Nevada mountains 8
Silicon Valley 47, *47*
slavery 10, 11, 11
smogs 34, 36, 37, 63
social data 60
   Mexico 32, 33
   USA 32, 33
soil erosion 50–1
solar power 48, 49
South Dakota Badlands *26*
states *10*, 11
   climate data 9
   minority populations *29*
   population density 26
Sun Belt 31, *40*, 41, 46, 63
Sunshine State see Florida

temperature ranges 8, 9, 54, 56, 63
Texas 29, 32, 48, 50, 51
theme and leisure parks 41, 57
Three Mile Island 49
time zones 4, 5
Tornado Valley 17
tornadoes 16–17, *17*
tourism 6, 25, 41, 47, 56, 58, 59
   trade 52–3, 61
   trade wars 53
trading partners 52

urbanization 31, 63

Vail, Colorado 7, *7*
Valmeyer, Illinois 23
vegetation 8, *8*, 9, 24
volcanic activity 14–15, *14*, 55
   composite volcanoes 14, *15*, 62
   shield volcanoes 14, 63

water conservation 20, 21
water resources 18–21, 51
   groundwater supplies 20, 21
wetlands 24–5, 63
wildlife 19, 24, 25, 54, 55
World Heritage Sites 25
Wyoming 18

Yellowstone National Park 6, 7, *7*
Yosemite 6
Yukon river 55